LIVING *through* HISTORY

Foundation Edition

the Making of the United Kingdom

Fiona Reynoldson
and
David Taylor

Heinemann

Heinemann Educational
Halley Court, Jordan Hill, Oxford OX2 8EJ
a division of Reed Educational and Professional
Publishing Ltd

OXFORD MADRID ATHENS FLORENCE
PRAGUE CHICAGO PORTSMOUTH NH (USA)
MEXICO CITY SAO PAULO SINGAPORE
KUALA LUMPUR TOKYO MELBOURNE
AUCKLAND IBADAN NAIROBI KAMPALA
GABORONE JOHANNESBURG

Heinemann is a registered trademark of
Reed Educational and Professional
Publishing Ltd.

First published 1998

00 99 98
10 9 8 7 6 5 4 3 2 1

British Library cataloguing in Publication data
for this title is available from the British Library.

ISBN 0 435 30977 3

Designed and produced by Dennis Fairey
and Associates Ltd.

Illustrated by John James, Arthur Phillips,
and Stephen Wisdom.

Special thanks to the Hengrave Hall Community
for their enthusiastic assistance. Educational R.E.
and History Days for Schools are provided by
the Community in the Tudor Hall throughout
the year. For further information contact:
Schools Project Organiser, Hengrave Hall Centre,
Bury St Edmunds, IP28 6LZ, or telephone
01284 701561.

Photographic acknowledgements

The authors and publisher would like to
thank the following for permission to
reproduce photographs:

Cover photo: AKG/Erich Lessing

Blair Castle Collection, Perthshire: 4.2A
Bridgeman Art Library: 1.1B, 2.2C, D, 5.2B,
5.4C, 5.9E, p. 87, 7.3A, 7.4B, E
Bridgeman Art Library/British Library: 6.2C
Bridgeman Art Library/Museum of London: 7.5A
Bridgeman Art Library/Scottish National Portrait
Gallery: 6.2B
British Library: 5.6A
British Museum: 4.3B
Cambridge University Library, Rare Books
Division: 7.5B
Master and Fellows, Corpus Christi College,
Oxford: 3.6A
ET Archive/Kobal Collection: 3.2A
Mary Evans Picture Library: 4.3A, 5.9B, 7.1A, E
Fotomas Index: 1.3D, 1.6C, 3.3B, 4.2C, 5.2C
Friends of Burford Church: 5.7A, B
Robert Harding Picture Library: 7.3E
Hengrave Hall Centre: 1.2B, 1.8A, B, G,
3.3A, 3.4C
House of Commons Education Unit: 2.1A
Hulton Deutsch Collection: 5.5B
Hulton-Getty Picture Collection Library: 1.6B
The Earl of Leicester and Trustees of the
Holkham Estate, Norfolk: 3.1A
Mansell Collection/Time Inc.: 6.1B
Methuen Collection: 2.2E
Trustees of the National Gallery: 1.5B
National Portrait Gallery, London: 1.1C, 1.3A,
p. 37, 3.6C, 5.9A
National Trust Photographic Library: 1.4A, 1.7B
Lord Petre, Ingatestone Hall, Essex: 2.1E
Pinacoteca Nazionale, Sienna: 2.2B
The Royal Collection © Her Majesty the Queen:
2.1B, 2.2A. 5.1A
Trustees of the Tate Gallery, London: 1.8F
Victoria and Albert Museum Picture Library,
London: 5.8A

The publishers have made evey effort to trace
copyright holders of material in this book.
Any omissions will be rectified in subsequent
printings if notice is given to the publisher.

CONTENTS

It was difficult being a king or queen. Other people wanted to be powerful too.

In 1485 Henry VII defeated Richard III at the Battle of Bosworth Field. Henry VII became the first Tudor king.

The Tudor kings and queens

- Henry VII
- Henry VIII
- Edward VI
- Mary
- Elizabeth I

End of the Tudors

Elizabeth I had no children. So her cousin became king when she died. He was called James Stuart.

The Stuart kings and queens

- James I (James Stuart)
- Charles I
- Parliament ruled
- Charles II
- James II
- William and Mary
- Anne.

Source A

King Henry VIII talking to a diplomat from Venice. He was trying to see if he looked more manly than his rival, the King of France.

His majesty asked 'Is the King of France as tall as I am?'

I replied 'He is about the same'.

He then asked 'Is he fat?'

I answered 'No he isn't'.

Henry finally asked 'Does he have strong legs? Look at my legs. Aren't they the legs of a fit and athletic man?'.

Parliament

Parliament was made up of several hundred rich men. They were called **Members of Parliament (MPs)**. They met to talk. They talked about what the king or queen should do.

Sometimes they said he or she should go to war. Other times they said that too much money was spent by the king or queen.

What Members of Parliament wanted

Most of all the Members of Parliament wanted the king or queen to listen to what they said. Quite often this annoyed kings like Charles I.

Source B

Henry VIII.

James II.

Everyday life

Most people lived by farming. They kept cows, sheep and other animals. They grew wheat and vegetables. Very rich people had servants to farm for them.

A few people worked as merchants. They bought and sold things like leather, wine and cloth. A very few people sailed to discover new lands. Some made lots of money by bringing back all sorts of spices and gold and silver to sell.

The king or queen, together with the Church, were very powerful. (Although sometimes it was more like arm wrestling.)

The rows got so bad that King Charles I went to war against Parliament. Parliament won. And Parliament chopped the king's head off.

Religion

Religion was very important. Almost everyone believed in God. The Church was God's power on Earth. So almost everyone did what the Church said.

Changes in religion

Henry VII became king in 1485. Everyone was a **Catholic**. Then after Henry VIII, most people became **Protestant**. There were lots of arguments about religion all through the Tudors and Stuarts.

Questions

1 Who was the first Tudor king?

2 Who was the first Stuart king?

3 What did Parliament do to Charles I?

4 When Henry VII became king everyone was Catholic. What religion did most people become after Henry VIII?

5 How did most people make their living at this time?

6 What can we learn about Henry VIII from Source A?

Choosing religion or not

There are many different religions in Britain today.

Religion in Tudor times

In early Tudor times there was only one religion in Britain – Christianity. And every Christian was in the Catholic Church. It was the only Church. It was headed by the **Pope**. He lived far away in Rome.

The church in the village

The church building was large. It was often in the middle of the village. Everyone went to church on Sunday to pray and think about God. At other times there were dances and feasts in the main part of the church.

Pictures in the church

There were lots of pictures in the church. Some were painted on the walls. Some were in glass in windows. The pictures showed good people who loved God. They also showed what happened to bad people. They went to Hell.

The Church became rich

Some people said that the Church had become too rich. It was too powerful. They said that some bishops and priests were lazy or wanted money. They were no longer good people at all. They did not follow the way of Jesus Christ.

The Pope

The Pope was the head of the Church. Some people said that Popes were not always good men. They liked money. Some Popes sold jobs in the Church to rich men.

Other people said that the Pope was a foreigner. He should not tell people in England what to do.

Source A

A report on a monastery in 1535.

Many of the monks devote themselves to hunting and shooting arrows.

The abbot is often drunk.

Some of the monks spend their time gambling with dice.

This church window shows Hell as the mouth of a monster.

Source B

The Reformation

Many people all over Europe wanted to reform or change the Church. They wanted the Church to be more simple and pure. One of these reformers was Luther, who lived in Germany.

Several other countries had a Reformation. They changed their Church and became Protestant.

The Reformation in England

Under Henry VIII, England changed religion from Catholic to Protestant.

How the Church was organised in early Tudor times

The picture below shows how the Church was organised in early Tudor times. Later, Henry VIII got rid of abbots, priors, monks, nuns and the Pope.

Questions

1 What was the only religion in early Tudor times?

2 a Who was head of the Catholic Church?
   b What complaints did people have about this person?

3 Write down four reasons why people went to the church in the village.

4 Look at Source B. What does the picture show?

5 Why do you think the men who ran the Church wanted pictures like this in churches?

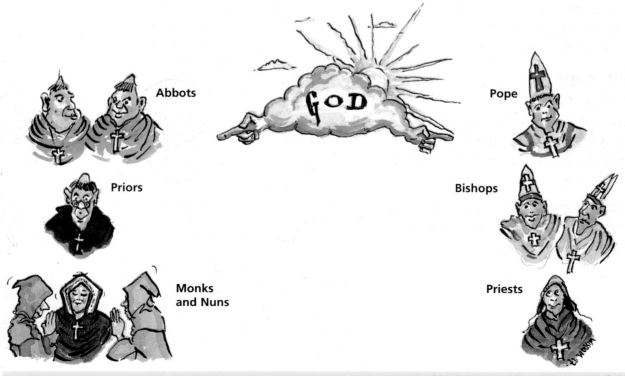

How the Church was organised in Tudor times.

1.3 HENRY VIII AND THE BREAK WITH THE POPE

Henry VIII

Henry VII died in 1509. His son, Henry VIII, became king. Henry VIII married Catherine of Aragon. They were happily married.

Henry and religion

Henry was religious. He supported the Catholic Church. He also supported the Pope, who was head of the Catholic Church.

Henry needed a son

Henry said he must have a son to be king after him. If he had a daughter, she would not be strong enough to control England.

Source A

Anne Boleyn.

Source B

I must have a son!

Only a daughter

It was 1527. Henry and Catherine had been married for many years. But they only had one daughter. Her name was Mary. Henry was desperate for a son. Catherine was too old to have any more children. So Henry said he must have a divorce from her.

Henry and the divorce

Henry asked the Pope for a divorce from Catherine. But the Pope was in a difficult position. He was being held prisoner by Catherine's nephew, Emperor Charles V. Charles V was angry and told the Pope to say 'no' to the divorce. Henry was furious.

Henry in love

Meanwhile, Henry had fallen in love with Anne Boleyn. She became pregnant in 1533. All the astrologers told Henry it would be a boy. Now Henry had to marry Anne quickly. But how could he get rid of Catherine?

Henry went against the Pope

The Pope would not give Henry a divorce. So Henry decided to go against the Pope. The leading churchman in the country was Thomas Cranmer. He was the Archbishop of Canterbury. Henry told Cranmer to let him have a divorce.

The divorce

Cranmer, as Archbishop of Canterbury, gave Henry a divorce from his wife, Catherine of Aragon.

Henry and Anne

Then Henry married Anne Boleyn. He waited for his baby to be born. Everyone was sure it would be a son. But it was a daughter. She was called Elizabeth.

Henry was bitterly disappointed.

Henry's six wives, his reasons for marrying them, and how the marriages ended.

Source C

A foreign visitor describes Anne Boleyn.

Anne has a brown face, long neck and wide mouth.

She has the king's affection.

Her eyes are big and black.

She has black hair which she wears loose.

Questions

1 Who was Henry VIII married to for many years?

2 Why didn't Henry want a daughter?

3 What was the name of Henry and Anne's daughter?

The end of Anne Boleyn

Anne had another baby. But it died. She had no more living children. So that was the end of Anne. Henry said she was a witch and had many lovers. Then he had her head chopped off.

Henry married again. This time he had a son (Edward). But what was Henry going to do about his row with the Pope?

Henry as Supreme Head of the Church

Henry wanted to be head of the Church, instead of the Pope. The Members of Parliament also wanted to be free of the Pope. So Parliament said it would make Henry the Supreme Head of the Church in England.

Now Henry was in charge of the Church. He was pleased.

Henry and Thomas More

Thomas More was an important Catholic. He said that Henry was wrong. He must not go against the Pope and the Catholic Church. But Henry had Thomas More executed.

Henry and the monasteries

Many people said the monasteries were not good and holy any more. Also, the monasteries had lots of money and land.

Henry had started to attack the Church because it had made it so difficult to divorce Catherine of Aragon. It was very easy for him to go on attacking the Church. He wanted the monasteries and land.

Source D

A picture from the time, showing Henry trampling on the Pope.

Questions

1 What did Parliament say it would make Henry?

2 a Who was Thomas More?
  b What happened to him?

3 How many monasteries were there in England and Wales?

4 What was the dissolution of the monasteries?

Henry and Thomas Cromwell

Henry made Thomas Cromwell his chief inspector. Together they sent men to inspect all 850 monasteries in England and Wales.

The men found that the 850 monasteries owned about a quarter of all the land in the country. They had lots of gold and silver too. The men also found that some monasteries did not do good work any more.

The dissolution of the monasteries, 1535–1539

Henry closed the monasteries. This was called the **dissolution of the monasteries**. Henry also shut down the nunneries, where nuns lived and worked. Henry sold their land and kept the money. Then he spent the money on wars.

A modern artist's impression of the scene where a nunnery was closed down.

1.4 FOUNTAINS ABBEY: THE FALL OF A GREAT MONASTERY?

What was Fountains Abbey?

Fountains Abbey was a big abbey in Yorkshire. It was very rich.

Many monks lived and worked in Fountains Abbey.

Fountains Abbey.

The story of Fountains Abbey

1132	The abbey was started.
1150–1200	Rich people gave money and land to the abbey.
	The monks farmed sheep and mined lead and iron.
1200–1265	The abbey became rich.
1300–1399	The monks ate meat very often.
	They paid servants to farm the land.
1536	The Abbot resigned.
	Marmaduke Bradley paid to become Abbot.
1539	The monks surrendered to the king.
1540	The abbey was stripped of its treasures and sold.

Rules at Fountains Abbey

The monks at Fountains lived by strict rules.

1 Monks had to:

- pray
- work (on the farm)
- study
- help the poor
- teach
- look after travellers.

2 Monks had to live far from a town.

3 Monks had to live from their farming.

4 Monks did not usually eat meat.

Source B

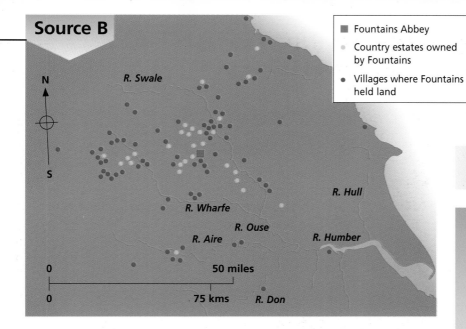

Legend:
- ■ Fountains Abbey
- ○ Country estates owned by Fountains
- ● Villages where Fountains held land

Map labels: R. Swale, R. Wharfe, R. Aire, R. Ouse, R. Hull, R. Humber, R. Don

N / S compass
0 — 50 miles
0 — 75 kms

Land owned by Fountains Abbey.

Source D

Robert Aske said that Henry VIII was wrong to close the monasteries.

The abbeys and monasteries gave money and food to poor people. They were beautiful places where men and women could serve God.

Source C

A report from an inspector of monasteries. It was sent to Thomas Cromwell in 1536.

The Abbot of Fountains Abbey has ruined the abbey, wasting his woodland and keeping six mistresses. He stole an emerald and a ruby from a gold cross. He has resigned.

There is a monk at the abbey called Marmaduke. He is wise. He will pay 600 marks (£400) to be made abbot.

Questions

1 Where was Fountains Abbey?

2 Read the **Rules of Fountains Abbey**.

Write out what the monks had to do.

3 Read Source C.

  a What had the abbot done?
  b Do you think that everything in the report was true? Give one reason why you might not believe the report.

4 Read Source D.

Robert Aske wanted the monasteries to stay open. Write down the two reasons he gave.

5 Read **The Story of Fountains Abbey**.

  a When was the abbey started?
  b When did the monks surrender to the King?
  c When was the abbey stripped of its treasures?

1.5 EDWARD VI: PROTESTANTISM STRENGTHENED

Edward VI became king

Henry VIII died in 1547.

The new king was his son, Edward. Edward was only nine years old.

Would England be Protestant or Catholic?

Henry had broken with the Pope. But he still had Catholic services in the churches. Many people wanted to go further. They wanted to be full Protestants (see the box on page 15).

Edward and the Duke of Northumberland

Edward was so young that a powerful man ruled for him. This man was called the Duke of Northumberland. The Duke was a Protestant. So he made England even more Protestant.

Edward VI fell ill

Edward fell ill with tuberculosis.

The Duke of Northumberland was very worried. If Edward died, Edward's sister Mary would be queen. Mary was a very strong Catholic.

Source A

The death of Lady Jane Grey.

The executioner gave her a handkerchief to tie round her eyes. He knelt and asked her to forgive him, which she did. She lay her head on the block and prayed.

Questions

1 When did Henry VIII die?

2 How old was Edward VI when he became king?

3 Which Duke controlled Edward VI?

4 What religion was this Duke?

5 What religion was Mary?

6 Why was Lady Jane Grey executed?

How England became Protestant under Edward VI

1547 Protestant books had to be read in all churches.

1548 All statues and paintings were taken from churches.

1549 All churches had to use the new Protestant prayer book. It was written by Archbishop Cranmer. Priests had to wear plain clothes.

A painting of the execution of Lady Jane Grey. It was painted in the nineteenth century.

The Duke of Northumberland's plot

The Duke of Northumberland had a plot. His daughter-in-law, Lady Jane Grey, was Henry VIII's niece. The Duke would make her queen.

Edward was dying. He agreed that Lady Jane Grey should be queen. But many powerful people did not like this. They thought that Mary was the rightful queen. After all, Mary was Henry VIII's daughter.

Mary became queen

The Duke of Northumberland was captured and beheaded. Mary became queen in 1553. England became Catholic again.

Soon after, Mary was worried that Lady Jane Grey might try to become queen. So Mary had Lady Jane beheaded.

Some differences between Catholics and Protestants

Catholic	Protestant
Church services were in Latin.	Church services were in English.
The Pope was head of the Church.	A king could be head of the Church.
What the Church said was true.	Only what the Bible said was true.
Churches should have statues and paintings.	Churches should be plain.
Priests wore colourful clothes.	Priests wore plain clothes.

Mary became queen

Mary became queen in 1553. England was used to having kings rule the country. A queen was a nice change from a king. Many people were pleased.

Mary and religion

But people were not pleased that Mary was a Catholic. She wanted everyone to be Catholic.

Bloody Mary

Mary had Protestants put to death. It was not long before people called her Bloody Mary.

What Mary did for Catholics

1 Catholic church services came back.

2 Protestant priests lost their jobs.

3 Mary tried to re-open monasteries.

   However, most of the land had been sold.

4 Mary married King Philip of Spain.

   Spain was a Catholic country.

5 In 1555 Mary had some important Protestants burnt to death. This was unpopular with many people. They felt it was very brutal.

Mary's life

Mary was born in 1516. Her mother was Catherine of Aragon. Her father was Henry VIII.

Henry divorced Catherine when Mary was eleven years old.

After her half brother Edward died, Mary became queen.

She had a younger half sister called Elizabeth.

Source A

From a diary at the time.

Mary became queen of England in July 1553. The bells rang out. There were bonfires and feasts in every street.

Source B

The burning of Thomas Cranmer in 1556. This was painted in the nineteenth century.

Source C

Another picture showing the burning of Thomas Cranmer.
This picture is in a best selling book from the time.

Source D

One Protestant bishop
comforted another.
They were both about
to be burnt.

**We shall this day light such
a candle by God's grace in
England as I shall trust shall
never be put out.**

Source E

This was written two days after Cranmer's burning. Before he was
burnt, Cranmer had signed some papers saying that he gave up
being a Protestant. Just before he died he went back on this.

**Cranmer put out his right hand into the flame and held it there
until his hand was seen on fire. He cried out 'This hand has
done wrong.'**

Source F

From a diary in 1558.

**Queen Mary died. All the
churches in London rang
their bells.**

That night bonfires were lit
and tables put in the streets
for eating and drinking.

Questions

1 When did Mary become queen?

2 Why were many people pleased about
Mary being queen?

3 What did Mary do to some Protestants?

4 Read **Mary's life**.

  a Write down the names of Mary's half brother
and half sister.

  b Look at the drawing of Henry VIII's six wives
on page 9. Write down the names of his first
three wives. These were the mothers of his
three children.

5 Read Source A.

  What things happened to celebrate when
Mary became queen?

6 Read Source F.

  Why do you think Mary was unpopular
by the time she died?

Elizabeth I was the daughter of Henry VIII and Anne Boleyn.

Elizabeth was a Protestant. But she was not strongly against the Catholics. She wanted a middle way.

Trouble with Catholics

A middle way was difficult. In 1569 some Catholics wanted England to be fully Catholic again. Elizabeth had the leaders executed. All seemed well. Then in 1570, the Pope said that Elizabeth was a wicked woman. All Catholics must rebel against her. They must get rid of her.

Support for Elizabeth

Lots of English people were angry. The Pope was a foreigner. They did not want him telling them what to do. They supported Elizabeth.

The law and Catholics

People said the law against Catholics must be harder. They did not want foreign Catholic priests coming to England.

Catholic priests had to hide in special **priestholes** (secret rooms) in Catholic people's houses. You can see one of these in Source B.

Trouble from Puritans

Puritans did not like Catholics. They wanted the Church to be even more Protestant than it was. They did not like the middle way. Puritans wanted the Church to be pure and simple (see the picture at top of page 19). They believed that everything must be plain.

Source A

What the Pope said in 1570.

Elizabeth, the pretended Queen of England, has said she is the Supreme Head of the Church in England.

We command everyone not to obey her.

What Queen Elizabeth said

I am Head of the Church.

Everyone must go to church or pay a fine.

Everyone must use the Protestant prayer book.

Catholic priests lose their jobs but none will be killed.

Priests can wear coloured clothes.

No music, statues or stained glass windows. No brightly coloured clothing, dancing, theatres or drinking to excess.

We want: long sermons based on the Bible, a God-fearing life, more schools and colleges, help for the poor.

What Puritans believed.

Source B

A priesthole.

Spain and England in the 1580s

Elizabeth was more worried about Spain than about the Puritans. The King of Spain was a strong Catholic. He agreed with the Pope. He wanted to get rid of Elizabeth and make England Catholic again.

The Spanish Armada, 1588

The Spanish sent a great fleet of ships to fight England. It was called the Spanish Armada. The English followed the Spanish up the English Channel. Then they fought and at last, a storm hit the ships.

The Spanish ships were blown north. Many were wrecked. Only half the ships got back to Spain. The danger to Elizabeth was over.

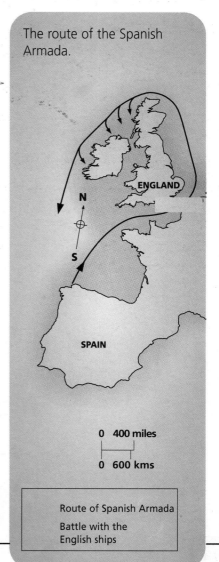

The route of the Spanish Armada.

N

S

ENGLAND

SPAIN

0   400 miles

0   600 kms

Route of Spanish Armada

Battle with the English ships

Questions

1 Who was Elizabeth I?

2 What religion was Elizabeth I?

3 Look at the picture about what Puritans believed on this page.

   a What did Puritans **not** want?
   b What did Puritans want?

4 When was the Spanish Armada?

5 What happened to the Spanish ships called the Armada?

1.8 THE KYTSONS: AN ELIZABETHAN FAMILY IN CRISIS?

Thomas Kytson – a rich merchant

Thomas Kytson was a rich **merchant**. He made a lot of money, buying and selling woollen cloth.

He built a beautiful, big house at Hengrave in Suffolk. It had a vineyard, fish ponds and gardens.

Thomas Kytson died in 1540. He left Hengrave to his widow. She was expecting a baby. The baby was a son. This was young Thomas Kytson.

Young Thomas Kytson gets married

When young Thomas Kytson grew up, he married Jane Paget. But she died within a year.

Young Thomas Kytson gets married again

Next he married Elizabeth Cornwallis. She came from a strong Catholic background. Young Thomas was also a Catholic. At first, young Thomas was not very careful about religion. He easily fell out with Elizabeth I (see Sources C and D).

Queen Elizabeth's visit in 1578

By 1578, young Thomas was in favour. Elizabeth visited him at Hengrave. She made him a knight (Sir Thomas Kytson).

Elizabeth's visit cost him a lot of money. He gave huge feasts for her and all her followers. He also gave her presents and put on shows.

Source A

Hengrave Hall as it is today.

A fashionable
Tudor gentleman.

The end of young Thomas – 1602

Thomas stayed a Catholic all his life. As long as he was not too open about it, Elizabeth did not mind. But there were times when he went too far. Both he and his wife spent some time in prison for being too open about their Catholic beliefs. But Elizabeth did not take away their possessions.

When Thomas died in 1602, he was still a very rich man.

Source B

The Kytson coat of arms.

Source C

A letter from young Thomas Kytson.

I understand I am accused of saying that the Queen does not care about religion.

I have never thought it and therefore certainly never said it.

I have been most unfairly slandered.

I beg you not to think badly of me.

Source D

A letter from young Thomas Kytson to Queen Elizabeth when she was first queen. He did not keep his promises.

I have been in prison since last September.

What I said then about religion was because I did not understand.

Now I want to obey the laws on religion. I will not be lazy in listening to sermons, reading books on religion and listening to wise men talk about religion.

Life at Hengrave

The Kytsons were rich. Elizabeth Kytson was in charge of running the house. This was a big job. She had servants to clean the house and do the washing. She had at least two cooks and other kitchen servants to make the meals.

Food

There was no running down to the shops to buy food. Most food was grown on the farm at home. A lot of food had to be stored so that it could be eaten in the winter time.

Food easily goes bad. There were no freezers or tins. Food had to be salted, dried, pickled and so on.

How food was stored

- Flour was made from wheat grown on the farm. The flour was stored in big, wooden tubs. It was used to make bread.

- Meat was salted in barrels.

- Vegetables were pickled.

- Fruit was preserved, often in sugar.

- Honey was collected from beehives.

- Herbs were dried.

Farm work

Women servants usually milked the cows, and made butter and cheese. They also looked after the hens.

Source E

From the account books at Hengrave.

Sums of money have to be paid for:

- **books for Margaret and Mary**

- **making silk dresses**

- **a bear man for bringing his bears to perform**

- **money lost in gambling by the master.**

Source F

LADY KYTSON

Elizabeth Kytson. She was a strong person. Her father asked her to sort out family quarrels.

The tomb of Thomas and Elizabeth Kytson in the local Protestant church.

The first wife of Thomas Kytson, Jane Paget, is also on the tomb. But notice how she has been pushed into the corner.

Farming the land

There was a lot of land at Hengrave. Many farm workers worked in the fields, the gardens and the vineyard. There were also men to look after the horses and other animals, ponds and gardens.

Entertainment

The Kytsons were rich. They had lots of people to visit. They feasted and they entertained. Music was very popular – the Kytsons kept a band of musicians at Hengrave Hall all the time.

Source H

Elizabeth Kytson helped the poor.

From 1625 Elizabeth gave £30 a year for houses for the poor.

From 1626 she gave £4 a year for new clothes for twelve poor people.

Questions

1 Where was most of the Kytsons' food grown?

2 How was meat stored?

3 Read Source E.

  Name two sorts of entertainment apart from music.

4 The Kytsons were always Catholics. Look at Source G. How does this show that they kept in with the Protestant religion?

5 Why do you think the statue of Jane Paget on the tomb in Source G has been pushed into the corner?

Parliament today

Parliament is made up of:

- the House of Commons (nearly 700 Members of Parliament)
- the House of Lords
- the Queen.

The **House of Commons** is the most powerful part of Parliament. It makes the laws. It also agrees how much money is given in taxes by ordinary people.

The **House of Lords** gives advice and agrees the laws.

The Queen signs the laws.

Voting

Nearly everyone who is over eighteen years old votes for a Member of Parliament. When people vote it is called a **general election**.

Tudor parliaments

Parliament was made up of the king or queen, the House of Lords and the House of Commons (about 300 Members of Parliament).

The king or queen ran the country. There were twenty or thirty rich, powerful lords who helped. The king or queen only asked the House of Commons to meet when they had to. That was usually when the king or queen needed more money to fight a war. Also, only the whole of Parliament together could pass new laws.

How Parliament could get more powerful.

Source A

Parliament in the 1990s.

Parliament under Henry VII

Parliament was not powerful under Henry VII.

Henry was a careful king. He did not want new laws and he did not want to fight wars.

Henry just wanted to rule as king.

Henry hardly ever called Parliament to meet.

Parliament under Henry VIII

Henry VIII was quite different to Henry VII. He wanted to pass laws to change religion. He also wanted to fight wars.

Henry kept calling Parliament to meet. The 300 Members of Parliament came to London for weeks on end. Often they wanted to go home. But changing England's religion was important. They passed law after law.

Source B

Henry VIII sitting at the head of Parliament.

Questions

1 How many Members of Parliament are there in the House of Commons today?

2 How many Members of Parliament were there in the House of Commons in Tudor times?

3 Give two reasons why Tudor kings and queens had to call parliaments.

Edward and Mary

Both Edward and Mary had to call Parliament

1 to pass laws, and

2 to give money.

Elizabeth had to call Parliament when she became queen for the same reasons.

Elizabeth I and Parliament

For most of the time, Elizabeth lived on her own money. She had about £200,000 a year. The money came from rent (she owned a lot of land), customs duties and so on. But sometimes Elizabeth needed more money:

• She needed money for war against Spain.

• She needed money to pay for ships and guns and soldiers.

• She needed more money to run the country.

Elizabeth and law

Sometimes Elizabeth needed to pass laws. There were laws about how to treat the poor, and laws about religion and so on.

Elizabeth and Parliament

Under Henry VIII, Parliament had got used to meeting more often. The Members of Parliament wanted a say in what laws were made and how the country was run. They knew Elizabeth needed money from them. So she had to listen.

Parliament wanted all sorts of new laws on religion. But Elizabeth said no. Parliament also wanted to tell the Queen who to marry. She told them to mind their own business. But the battle went on. If the Queen said no too often, Parliament would not give her any money.

Source C

Written by a modern historian.

Elizabeth only called Parliament thirteen times in the forty-four years of her reign.

For Elizabeth, Members of Parliament were little boys. They were a waste of an intelligent woman's time.

Source D

For everyday work, Elizabeth had advisers. They met several times a week. They worked on things like helping English merchants abroad, stopping new building in London and training soldiers.

The most important advisers in the middle of Elizabeth's reign were:

• **Lord Burghley**

• **Earl of Leicester**

• **Sir Francis Knollys**

• **Earl of Lincoln**

• **Sir Francis Walsingham**

• **Sir Christopher Hatton**

• **Sir James Croft.**

Running the country – Sir William Petre

Kings and queens needed people to run the country every day. This was Sir William Petre's job. He was born in 1506. He studied law and was a friend of Anne Boleyn's father. He got a job working on Henry VIII's divorce. He did other jobs for the King and became a Member of Parliament too.

Sir William Petre and Edward VI

After Henry died, Sir William worked for young King Edward. One of his jobs was to talk to Princess Mary. He had to try and get her to give up being a Catholic. He also checked on books that were published. No Catholic books were allowed.

Sir William Petre and Mary

Edward died and Sir William worked for Queen Mary. But he retired in 1553 because he was not very well. After that, he worked part time.

Sir William Petre and Elizabeth

Sir William worked for Queen Elizabeth for a little while. But he was not well. He wrote to a friend in 1565: *I have recovered from fever but am still a little deaf. I shall take medicine for the pain from my head to my shoulders.*

Sir William died in 1572. His wife was a Catholic. She built priestholes at the family home.

This was a very unusual thing for her to do. One of her husband's jobs had been to stop the Catholic religion from spreading.

Source E

Sir William Petre.

Questions

1 How often did Elizabeth call parliaments?

2 Why did Elizabeth tell the Members of Parliament to mind their own business?

3 When was Sir William Petre born?

4 How many kings and queens did Sir William Petre work for?

Very few people wrote about what Elizabeth I looked like.

Pictures of Elizabeth

There are quite a lot of pictures of Elizabeth. But kings and queens always wanted to look good. They did not pay painters to make them look weak and ugly.

Elizabeth made sure that paintings showed her looking good.

There was no television or newspapers then, and travel was difficult. So few people would ever see the Queen.

Source A

Elizabeth as a young girl in 1546.

Source B

Elizabeth in 1583.

Source C

Elizabeth in 1600.

Source D

Elizabeth in 1588.

Source E

Elizabeth in about 1600, but painted after her death in 1603.

Source F

An order made in 1563.

No one will paint a picture of the Queen until a very good painter has painted her picture.

Then all other painters must paint the Queen in the same way.

Source G

A foreigner described Elizabeth in 1574.

She is tall and well formed with a good skin, though rather dark. She has fine eyes.

Source H

Another foreigner described Elizabeth in 1598.

Her face is good-looking but wrinkled. Her eyes are small, black and pleasant. Her nose is hooked, her lips narrow. She has a red wig.

Questions

1 Look at Sources A–E.

  a Write one sentence to describe what Elizabeth looks like in each of the pictures.

  b How old do you think she looks in each picture? (Just put **young** or **old**.)

2 Elizabeth was born in 1533 and died in 1603. Write down how old she was in each picture.

3 Which picture is:

  a most real looking

  b most unreal looking?

  Give one reason for each of your answers.

4 Read Source H.

  What two things tell you that Elizabeth is quite old by this time?

Life in the country

Most people lived in villages in the country. They worked on the land in big, open fields. A few rich people did not have to work in the fields. They paid workers to farm for them.

A new way of farming – enclosure

The old way of farming was in big fields that everyone shared. The new way of farming was in small fields that were fenced in. These fields were not shared. This way of farming with small fields was called **enclosure**. More and more farmers wanted enclosure in Tudor times.

Hard work and leisure

The farm workers worked from dawn to nightfall. They ploughed. They sowed seed. They cut the wheat. They looked after the animals. But they did have some holidays (holy days). One holiday was May Day. There was dancing and drinking and football.

The size of towns

The biggest town in Tudor times was London, which had 100,000 people. The next biggest towns were Norwich, Bristol and York. But none of these had more than 20,000 people – the size of a small town today.

Houses in the towns

Houses in the towns were jammed close together. Sometimes people could touch each other across the street from their top windows.

Source A

Work in a Tudor village.

Filthy towns

The towns were filthy. There were no flushing toilets. All rubbish and human waste went into the street or river. Many people died from diseases.

Markets

Big towns had markets. Farmers and their families came to towns and sold sheep, cows, eggs and milk in the market.

There were shops all round the market. There were shoe menders, barbers, dentists and lots of pubs. Market day was a good time to meet friends, have a drink and buy some things in the town.

Questions

1 Where did most people live?

2 What was enclosure?

3 Why were the towns filthy?

4 Why was market day a good time for some people?

There were four sorts of doctors:

1 Physicians

Physicians were the top doctors. They were trained at university. They studied for many years. They charged a lot of money.

2 Barber surgeons

Barbers cut hair. So many people thought they must be good at cutting off arms and legs too. (There were no **anaesthetics** then.) Physicians looked down on barber surgeons. They thought they were like butchers.

3 Apothecaries

Apothecaries mixed up medicines for physicians. They also sold the medicines themselves. They did not charge as much as physicians.

4 Midwives

Women were not allowed to go to university. A woman was allowed to be a midwife. A midwife delivered babies.

Treating illness

The ways of treating illness were often very different from today.

However, some common sense things, like resting if you were ill, were the same.

Many people believed that a king or queen could cure diseases like **scrofula** by touch.

Medicine and the Greeks

Many physicians used Greek ideas in medicine. The Greeks said there were four **humours** in the body. The four humours were:

- yellow bile
- black bile
- blood
- phlegm.

If the four humours were out of balance, a person became ill. For instance, if a person had too much blood, a physician made a cut and took some out.

Source A

Medicine and the stars

Many people believed in **astrology**. They said the moon and stars affected illness.

Everyday medicine

We do not know about everyday medicine for ordinary people. No one wrote it down.

Many people were treated by mothers, grandmothers and local wise women. They had a knowledge of herbs passed down by word of mouth.

Source B

A Tudor cure for **tuberculosis**.

Take a nine day old pig. Add spearmint, turnip, celery, nine dates and cinnamon. Cook. Put the juice in a glass in the sun for nine days. Drink nine spoonfuls.

Source C

From the account book at Hengrave Hall in 1573.

Reward for letting my mistress' blood 2 shillings.

LADY GRACE MILDMAY

Growing up

Lady Grace Mildmay was born in 1552. She was brought up strictly.

Marrying

Lady Grace married Anthony Mildmay in 1567. He was not keen on the marriage. He spent a lot of time away from home.

Lady Grace's day

Lady Grace spent her time reading the Bible, playing the lute, sewing and looking after sick people.

Lady Grace and medicine

Lady Grace became very interested in medicine. She grew herbs and made medicines. She kept a notebook of the herbs she used. That is how we know about her work.

Lady Grace became very skilled. She treated everything from **smallpox** and skin disease to unwanted pregnancies.

Questions

1 a Write down the four sorts of doctors in Tudor times.
  b Write down what each one did.

2 Write three sentences about Lady Grace Mildmay.

3 How do we know about Lady Grace Mildmay's use of herbs?

4 Why do you think the mistress of Hengrave Hall (Source C) paid someone to 'let' her blood?

The number of poor people increased in Tudor times. There were three reasons for this:

1 There were a million more people by the year 1600. So there were more people looking for work, and there was not enough food.

2 Farmers kept more of their sheep in the new enclosures (small fields). One shepherd could look after a lot of sheep. So there were fewer jobs.

3 More people wanted to buy more things, so prices went up. Poor people were left behind.

Source A

These houses were built at Hengrave Hall for family servants and the deserving poor.

What rich people thought

Some rich people were afraid when they saw lots of poor people. They thought the poor people might try to attack them, or steal their things.

There were two types of poor people:

1 The deserving poor

Some people could not help being poor. They were too sick, too old or too young to work. People thought they should help them.

2 Sturdy beggars

These were people who were fit and well, but who did not want to work. Some of them wandered from village to village. They begged or worked a bit. Many people thought they should be punished.

Punishments

Because rich people were afraid of them, sturdy beggars were often punished severely. Some were **branded** on the ear. Others were whipped in the street. If they carried on begging, they might even be hanged.

What did the government do?

The government wanted to help the deserving poor. It passed some laws in Parliament:

1572 The rich must pay some money to help the deserving poor.

1597 Sturdy beggars found wandering must be whipped and sent back to their home village.

1601 Towns and villages must collect money to help the deserving poor.

Source B

A sturdy beggar being whipped.

Source C

This story comes from a book of 1567. We do not know if it is true.

Nicholas Jennings the beggar

Nicholas Jennings was begging in London. He was dressed in rags and covered in blood and dirt.

Found out by two boys

Two boys saw him smear the blood and dirt on himself. They fetched a constable. Nicholas had lots of money on him (twenty times as much money as a good worker could earn in a day).

Nicholas washed

When Nicholas was washed, they found he was fit and well.

Source D

From the account books of Hengrave Hall. Gifts to the poor.

To old John	**12 pence**
To the collector of the poor	**12 pence**
For a pair of shoes for a servant boy	**13 pence**

Questions

1 Write down the three reasons why the number of poor people increased in Tudor times.

2 **a** How many sorts of poor people were there?
  b Who were the deserving poor?
  c Who were sturdy beggars?

3 Look at all the sources. Which sources tell you some people were kind to the poor?

Explorers

Explorers are people who look for new lands. In Tudor times many men sailed from England and Europe to find new lands. Christopher Columbus was a famous explorer. He discovered the West Indies. You can see this in the map below.

Merchants

Exploring was exciting. But there was money to be made too. Merchants are people who buy and sell all sorts of things from fish to gold.

What merchants wanted

Merchants wanted to buy silk, jewels and spices from the East. They wanted to buy furs and wood from Russia. They could sell all these things in England.

Merchants and slaves

Sometimes they bought and sold people as **slaves**. They bought them in Africa and sold them in the West Indies.

Selling English wool

It was all very well buying things. But merchants had to sell things too. They sold English wool all over the world.

Where English wool went

Clothes made from English wool went as far away as China and India. Men like Thomas Kytson of Hengrave Hall made a lot of money from selling wool.

Source A

From the Johnson Letters. The Johnsons were Tudor merchants. These are some things they had bought to sell in England.

My master has asked me to write thanking you for the parcels.

12 lb pepper

1 lb cloves

1/2 lb mace

I lb grains

I lb nutmeg

2 lb ginger

1 green carpet

1 lb cinnamon

1 box fruit in sugar

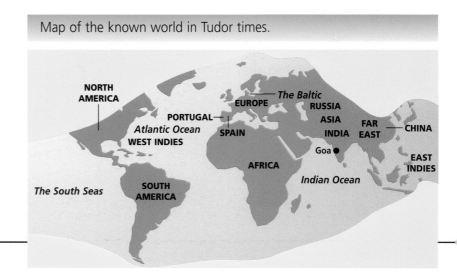

Map of the known world in Tudor times.

Wars

Many countries wanted to own new lands. Then their merchants could buy and sell things in these new lands.

This meant that countries like England and Spain went to war about who should own new lands.

Source B

Written by a Spanish spy in England in 1586.

Francis Drake has returned from the Indies. He captured several of our towns. He took 140 cannons, £1,000 of pearls, £70,000 of gold and silver.

Source C

A carving at Hengrave Hall. The figure of Death is wearing a woollen **shroud**. Queen Elizabeth ordered that everyone must be buried in woollen shrouds. This meant more wool was sold.

Questions

1 What is an explorer?

2 Find the names of two famous explorers on these pages.

3 What is a merchant?

4 What sort of things did Tudor merchants buy?

5 What did Tudor merchants sell all over the world?

SIR FRANCIS DRAKE

Sir Francis Drake was a great seaman and explorer. He attacked the Spanish in the West Indies (see map page 36).

He sailed round the world in 1577 in his ship the *Golden Hind*.

Elizabeth knighted him. (Made him Sir Francis Drake.)

He helped to defeat the Spanish Armada in 1588.

London people loved going to the **theatre**. At first actors put on plays in pubs and markets.

Theatres in London

Then James Burbage built a theatre in 1576. Soon there were several theatres. The Globe Theatre was a famous theatre.

There were also theatres called the Rose, the Swan and the Curtain. All the theatres were very much alike. They looked like the picture on this page. The centre part was open to the sky.

Putting on a play

The actors put up a flag if the weather was good enough for a play. People could see it from a long way away.

When a play was about to start, a trumpet was blown. Then, while the play was on a white flag flew over the theatre.

All the money for the tickets was kept in a box in a small office. We get the name 'box office' from this.

Watching a play

Poor people paid one penny. They stood in front of the stage. Richer people sat further back. Food and drink was on sale all the time. People laughed and talked. If they did not like the play they threw rotten eggs at the actors.

There were always a lot of pickpockets about. This made many people think that theatres were dangerous and wicked places.

Writers

William Shakespeare (1564–1616) is still the most famous writer of plays in the world. He wrote 38 plays. These include *Romeo and Juliet*. Christopher Marlowe was another famous writer.

Actors

There were usually about twelve actors in a play.

All the actors were male. Boys played the part of women. Most groups of actors had a patron. The patron was an important rich person. He helped the group of actors by giving them money.

Source A

This was written by a Puritan in 1518.

One trumpet blow brings 1,000 people to watch a play. While a church bell only brings 100 to church.

Source B

From a diary in the 1590s.

If more than 30 people a week die of the plague in London all the theatres will be closed.

Source C

London people walked across London Bridge to watch a play at the Globe Theatre. It was about a ten minute walk.

Questions

1 Where did actors put plays on at first?

2 What did William Shakespeare and Christopher Marlowe do?

3 Read Source B.

Why do you think the theatres were closed if there were a lot of people dying of the plague?

It was 30 May 1593. Four men, including Christopher Marlowe, met at a house near London. They spent the day talking. No one knows what it was about.

Then, in the evening, a row broke out. Marlowe hit one of the others on the head with the handle of a dagger. They fought. Somehow the dagger stabbed Marlowe in the right eye. He died instantly.

This may be a picture of Marlowe when he was twenty-one years old.

Source A

Who were the four men?

All four men were probably government spies. They did jobs such as spying on English Catholics in France and in England.

One of the four men worked for Thomas Walsingham, who helped his cousin run the secret spy service for Queen Elizabeth. Christopher Marlowe himself worked as a spy.

Was Marlowe's death an accident or murder?

The man who stabbed Marlowe was let off. It was called self-defence. But only the four men in the room knew what really happened.

Marlowe was an atheist. An atheist is someone who says there is no God. This was very serious in Tudor England.

If Marlowe was found guilty of being an atheist, he would have been tortured and then killed.

What might Marlowe have said under torture? He might have given away names of other atheists. Maybe someone wanted to make sure Marlowe never lived to do this.

Source B

From a modern history book, 1992.

Marlowe is remembered as a writer, an atheist, a homosexual and a man who lived fast and died young.

Marlowe's last days

18 May

Privy Council

Marlowe was accused of writing that there was no God.

18–30 May

Marlowe was allowed to go free. He had to report to the Privy Council every day.

30 May

The Privy Council got a report that Marlowe was an atheist and had important friends. If this was believed, Marlowe would be tortured and killed. He might give away the names of his important friends. **Who were they?**

30 May 6 p.m.

Marlowe was stabbed to death.

Source C

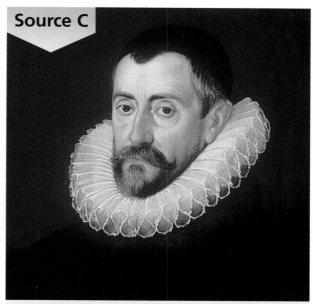

Francis Walsingham, who ran Queen Elizabeth's secret spy service.

Source D

This is from a report to the government about Christopher Marlowe.

Marlowe said that Christ was illegitimate, that Christ deserved to die and that, if there is a God or religion, it is the Catholics'.

Questions

1 What is an atheist?

2 How did Marlowe die?

3 Can you suggest any ideas about why he died?

Religion was very important to people during Tudor and Stuart times. Everyone believed in God and Jesus Christ.

Roman Catholics

Up to the reign of Henry VIII (1509–1547) everyone was a Roman Catholic. Henry broke away from the Catholic Church. He started the Church of England (or **Anglican Church**). Most people in England were now Protestants. The few Catholics left were forced to worship in secret.

Protestants

The Protestants in the Church of England split into two groups. Each group had its own idea about how to worship God.

- The Laudians wanted bishops and colourful churches.

- The Puritans wanted simple, plain churches and no bishops.

In the 1600s some Protestants left the Church of England. They included the Quakers and the Baptists. These groups were called **Dissenters** because they went against the Church of England.

Religious groups in the seventeenth century.

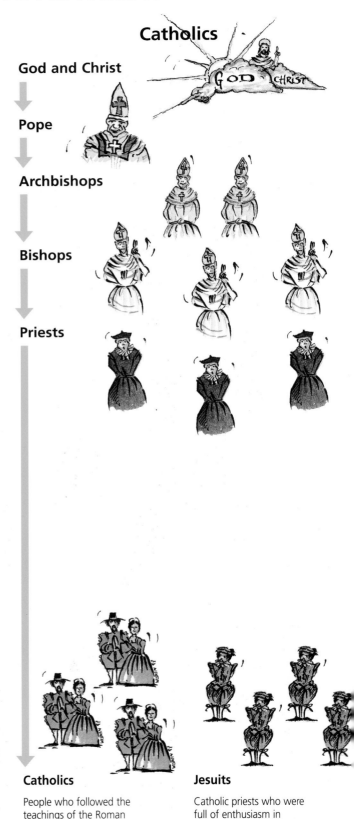

Catholics

God and Christ

Pope

Archbishops

Bishops

Priests

Catholics
People who followed the teachings of the Roman Catholic Church.

Jesuits
Catholic priests who were full of enthusiasm in following Catholic teachings and teaching others to do so.

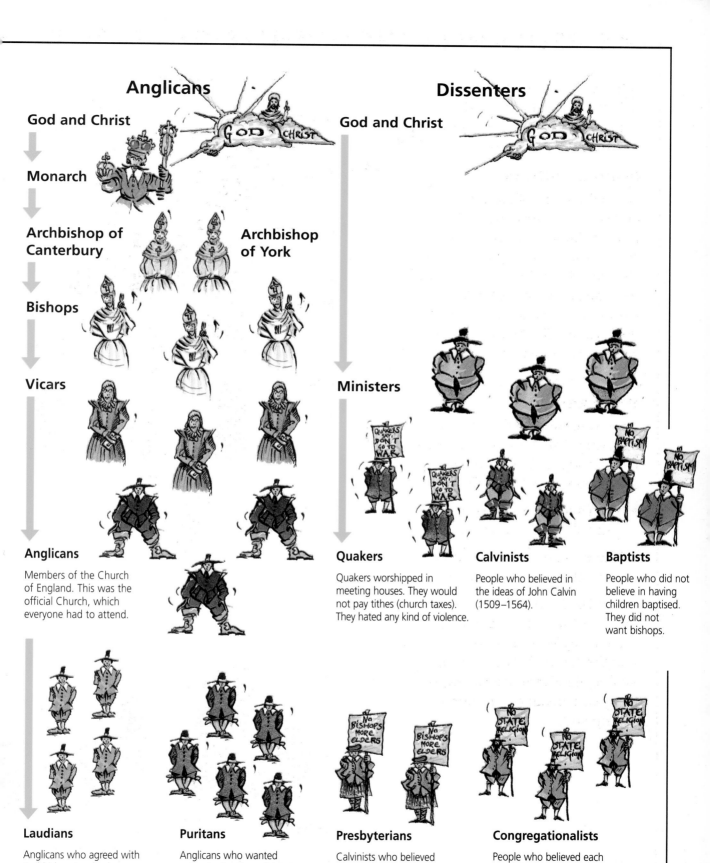

Anglicans

God and Christ

Monarch

Archbishop of Canterbury   **Archbishop of York**

Bishops

Vicars

Anglicans

Members of the Church of England. This was the official Church, which everyone had to attend.

Dissenters

God and Christ

Ministers

Quakers

Quakers worshipped in meeting houses. They would not pay tithes (church taxes). They hated any kind of violence.

Calvinists

People who believed in the ideas of John Calvin (1509–1564).

Baptists

People who did not believe in having children baptised. They did not want bishops.

Laudians

Anglicans who agreed with Archbishop Laud's changes. They wanted bishops and colourful churches.

Puritans

Anglicans who wanted a simple church service. They wanted theatres and horse-racing banned.

Presbyterians

Calvinists who believed that there should be no bishops. They ran the Church in Scotland.

Congregationalists

People who believed each congregation (group of worshippers) should choose its own officials and ministers.

A new king

Elizabeth I died in 1603. James I became the King of England.

High hopes

Both the Catholics and the Puritans hoped that James would be on their side. Both groups were left disappointed.

James I and Church matters

1 James I and the Catholics

James I was a Protestant. He did nothing to help the Catholics. He told Catholic priests to leave England. This made the Catholics angry.

2 James I meets the Puritans

In 1604 James I met the Puritans at Hampton Court. The Puritans said they did not want to have any bishops. But James did not agree. He sent the Puritans away. This made the Puritans angry.

3 A new Bible

In 1611 James I published a new Bible. It was written in English, not Latin. Now everyone could understand the Bible better.

Charles I

James I died in 1625. His son became king – Charles I.

Source A

James next to his mother Mary, Queen of Scots. It shows the year as 1583. But James never saw his mother again after 1567. The artist has made the picture up!

Source B

James I said this in 1604.

The Puritans must do as they are told, or I will chase them out of the country.

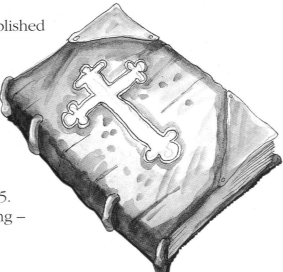

Source C

A cartoon drawn in 1637. It shows Laud with three Puritans who have had their ears cut off. One of the Puritans, William Prynne, is holding his head where his ears were. The ears are on a plate in front of Laud.

Source D

James I said this to Parliament in 1609.

Charles I agreed with what he said.

Kings are sent by God to rule over people.

No person on earth has more power than the King.

Parliament cannot tell the King what to do. Only God has more power than the King.

Charles I and Church matters

1 Archbishop Laud

In 1633 Charles I made William Laud the Archbishop of Canterbury. Charles and Laud made some changes to the Church of England. They said churches should have stained-glass windows and colourful paintings on the walls.

2 Laud and the Puritans

Puritans did not want these changes. So Laud banned Puritan books and had some Puritans put into prison. Others had their ears cut off (see Source C).

3 Puritans leave England

Some Puritans went to America. There they could worship in the way they wanted (see pages 48 and 49).

Trouble ahead!

Parliament did not like the changes that Laud and Charles I made to the Church. In the end, Charles and Parliament went to war.

Questions

1 Read page 44.

  Copy the sentences below. Choose one of the words in italics.

  James I made both the Catholics and the Puritans *happy/angry/delighted*. In 1611 James I published a new Bible. It was written in *Latin/English*.

2 Read **Charles I and Church matters**.

  a What changes did Charles I and Laud make to the Church of England?
  b Why did this anger the Puritans?
  c What did Laud do to the Puritans?
  d What did some Puritans do after this?

3 Read Source D.

  Did James I and Charles I believe that kings had more power or less power than Parliament?

Source A

> my lord out of the loue i beare ~~you~~ To some of youere freindz i haue a caer of youer preseruacion Therfor i would... aduyse yowe as yoube Tender youer Lyf To deuys some epscuse To shift of youer aHendance at This parleament

Part of the letter sent to Lord Monteagle on 4 November 1605.

It is telling him not to go to the Houses of Parliament.

Angry Catholics

Catholics were angry that James I had done nothing to help them. Catholics wanted to worship in their own way, but James I would not let them.

The plot

Some Catholics were so angry that they made up a plot.

James I had to open Parliament on 5 November 1605. The plot was to blow up the Houses of Parliament and kill James.

Gunpowder

The plotters rented a cellar underneath the Houses of Parliament. They hid thirty-six barrels of gunpowder in the cellar.

A letter

On 4 November, a Catholic called Lord Monteagle received a letter. It told him not to go to Parliament the next day.

Guy Fawkes

Lord Monteagle gave the letter to the government. Soldiers were sent to search the cellar.

The soldiers found Guy Fawkes and the gunpowder. Fawkes was tortured and owned up. The plotters were later executed.

Bonfires

People were angry when they heard about the plot. Now Catholics were hated more than ever. Protestants lit bonfires to show they were glad that the plot had failed.

Guy Fawkes' signature before and after he was tortured.

Source B

SUPPLICIUM

A print showing the execution of the gunpowder plotters.

Some of the gunpowder plotters.

Thomas Percy *Guy Fawkes* *Robert Catesby*

Questions

1 Read **Angry Catholics**.

Why were Catholics angry with James I?

2 Read **The plot** and **Gunpowder.**

What did some Catholics plan to do?

3 Read **A letter** and **Guy Fawkes**.

a What did the letter to Lord Monteagle say?

b What did he do?

c What did the soldiers do?

d What happened to Guy Fawkes?

4.4 PURITANS PROTEST: THE PILGRIM FATHERS, 1620

Unhappy Puritans

Many Puritans were unhappy with James I. He would not let them worship in the way they wanted to.

A new country – a new life

One group of Puritans decided to go to America. Here they could worship as they wanted. They would live simple lives. James I would not be able to bother them.

The journey

On 16 September 1620, a ship called the *Mayflower* set sail for America. There were 100 Puritans on board. They became known as the **Pilgrim Fathers**. Pilgrims are people who go on religious journeys.

The journey was terrible. The ship was too crowded. They soon ran out of fresh food.

There were lots of storms. Many of the Pilgrims were seasick. Some fell ill with diarrhoea.

On 20 December 1620, the *Mayflower* finally arrived in America.

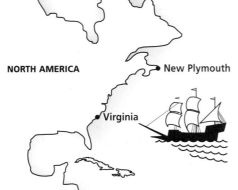

NORTH AMERICA — New Plymouth — Virginia

Source A

From a modern history book.

The Pilgrims called their town New Plymouth. They built a big wooden church there. Now they could worship God in peace.

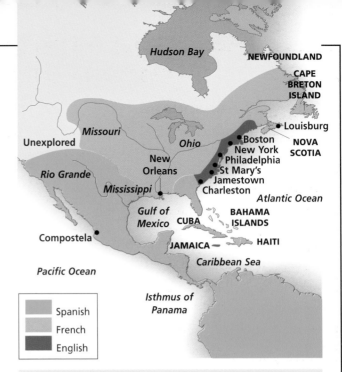

Spanish, French and English land in America before 1700.

Questions

1 Read **A new country – a new life**.

   Why did the Puritans go to America?

2 Read **Starting a new life**.

   Why were things hard to begin with?

3 Read **Help arrives**.

   How did the Indians help the Pilgrims to survive?

Starting a new life

Where the Pilgrims landed was cold and empty. They had to start a town from scratch. They built log houses to live in.

Life was hard to begin with. The Pilgrims planted seeds, but they did not grow. In the first year, half the Pilgrims died from illness or hunger. It looked as if they would all die.

Help arrives

Then some Indians showed them how to make the crops grow well. They planted corn, pumpkins and beans. The harvest of 1621 was very good. There was plenty of food.

The Pilgrims celebrated with the Indians. They feasted on roast turkey and goose, and they gave thanks to God for the harvest.

Soon they were joined by other Puritans from England.

5.1 JAMES I: THE WISEST FOOL IN CHRISTENDOM?

James VI of Scotland

James Stuart was born in 1566. He became King James VI of Scotland when he was just one year old!

James was an unhappy child. He was lonely and his teachers bullied him.

But James was very clever. He read lots of books and knew a lot of things. When he grew up, he turned out to be one of Scotland's best kings.

James I of England

Just before she died in 1603, Elizabeth I said she wanted James to become king.

James was very pleased to be the new King of England.

Most English people were pleased too. James was a Protestant and this was what they wanted.

As James travelled to London, people lined the way. They cheered and wished him luck.

Would James I be a good king?

James rides south to London.

Source A

James I of England.

Source B

Written by an Englishman in 1650.

James was fat. His eyes were large and rolling. His tongue was too large for his mouth. His drink used to dribble from his mouth. He never washed his hands. James was clever about small things, but a fool about things that mattered.

James I and Parliament

James believed that he was the most powerful person in the country. Only God had more power than him. He soon fell out with Parliament. Why was this?

1 James had money problems

James liked spending money. Parliament thought he spent too much and it would not let him raise taxes. James started to borrow money from banks. Parliament did not like this.

2 James had favourites

James chose his own ministers (people who helped him rule). His **favourite** minister was George Villiers, the Duke of Buckingham. James paid him lots of money and gave him presents. Parliament did not like this.

3 James told Parliament off

Parliament did not like the way James ran the country. James told Parliament to mind its own business. He said Parliament could not tell him how to run the country.

James was mistaken

Falling out with Parliament was a mistake. James should have realised that he needed Parliament's help to run the country well.

The wisest fool?

James I is often nicknamed the 'wisest fool in **Christendom**' (the part of the world where Christians lived). This is because he was clever, but he still made mistakes in running the country.

Source C

Written by a modern historian.

James I was clever. But he was soft with people. One minute he was telling them off, the next he gave in to them. He took too much notice of his favourites and could be big-headed.

Source D

James I said this in 1621.

Parliament has too much to say. I am surprised English kings have allowed this.

Questions

1 Make a bigger copy of this diagram.

Good  **Bad**

2 Read Source B and Source C.

   a Put James I's **good points** on your diagram.

   b Put James I's **bad points** on your diagram.

3 Read **James I and Parliament**.

   Write down three reasons why James fell out with Parliament.

4 Do you agree that James was 'the wisest fool in Christendom'? Explain your answer.

Charles I quarrels with Parliament

When James I died in 1625, his son Charles became king. Charles I soon fell out with Parliament. Why was this?

1 Money

Charles I spent a lot of money on his friends and on fighting wars against France and Spain. He kept asking Parliament for more money. But Parliament said he should cut down his spending.

2 Power

Charles believed he had the power to run the country without Parliament. He did not like Parliament telling him what to do.

Charles decides to rule on his own

Charles grew tired of Parliament's complaints. In 1629 he decided to rule by himself. Parliament did not meet again until 1640.

Ship Money

Charles needed to raise some money. Ship Money was an old tax that sea ports paid during wartime. The money was used to pay for the navy.

In 1635 there was no war on. But Charles said the whole country had to pay Ship Money. This made many people angry.

The *Sovereign of the Seas*, built in 1637. It was paid for out of Ship Money.

Source A

A **civil war** is when two sides from the same country fight each other.

King

V

Parliament

The English Civil War was between the King and Parliament.

Source B

John Hampden

John Hampden said that Ship Money was against the law and he would not pay it. Hampden was taken to court. The judges ordered him to pay, even though half of them agreed with him!

Charles I was becoming very unpopular.

Church matters again

Many Members of Parliament were Puritans. Charles brought back stained-glass windows in churches. He also allowed priests to wear colourful robes. The Puritans did not like this.

Charles angers the Scots

In 1637 Charles made a big mistake. He told the Scots to use the English Prayer Book in their churches. The Scots were furious.

Riots broke out during church services in Scotland. A Scottish army marched into England.

Without Parliament to vote him taxes, Charles had no money. He could not afford to raise an army to fight the Scots.

Charles was forced to call Parliament to ask for some money.

May 1640: Parliament meets

When Parliament met, it was in an angry mood. The Members of Parliament had not met for eleven years. They had lots of complaints about Charles.

The Members of Parliament said they would not give Charles any money, unless he listened to their complaints. But Charles would not listen. He ended Parliament after three weeks.

The Arch-Prelate of St Andrewes in Scotland reading the new Service-booke in his pontificall assaulted by men & women, with Cricketts stooles Stickes and Stones

A cartoon from 1637. It shows a riot in a Scottish church.

Questions

1 Read Source A. What is a civil war?

2 Read **Charles I quarrels with Parliament**.

What two things did Charles I and Parliament argue about?

3 Read **Charles angers the Scots**.

What made the Scots riot?

4 Read **May 1640: Parliament meets**.

Why did Parliament meet?

The Scots again

The Scots said they would go back to Scotland if Charles gave them some money. Charles agreed, even though he still did not have any money! He was forced to call Parliament again.

November 1640: Parliament meets again

The Members of Parliament were led by John Pym. They were still angry with Charles. Before they would give Charles any money, they made him agree to their demands.

Charles gives in

Charles agreed to:

- call Parliament every three years
- not tax people without asking Parliament first
- stop the changes made to the Church by William Laud.

Parliament now gave Charles money to pay off the Scots.

Laud and Strafford

The hated Laud was put in prison. Parliament said Thomas Strafford should be executed. (Strafford had helped Charles to run the country between 1629 and 1640.) Charles agreed to this.

Rebellion in Ireland

In 1641 Catholics in Ireland rebelled. Charles asked Parliament for money to raise an army against the Irish. But Parliament would not agree. It did not want Charles to be in charge of an army. He might use it to fight against Parliament.

A scene from the film *Cromwell*. Charles is looking for the five MPs.

Questions

1 Read **Civil War breaks out** on page 55.

   Why was the war fought?

2 Look at the diagram at the bottom of page 55.

   a What nickname was given to the King's side?

   b What nickname was given to Parliament's?

Charles loses his temper

Charles was especially fed up with John Pym and four other Members of Parliament. He decided to go to the Houses of Parliament and arrest them.

On 4 January 1642 Charles burst into Parliament with some soldiers. But the MPs had been warned. They were not there. Charles was angry and called out: *I see the birds are flown!*

Charles had been made to look very silly. Things between Parliament and Charles were very bad. They hated each other. Only a war would settle their quarrel.

Civil war breaks out

In August 1642 Charles raised his flag at Nottingham. This showed that he was at war with Parliament. Charles got an army together, and Parliament raised its own army to fight him.

The Civil War had begun. It was fought to see who should run the country: the King or Parliament.

The two sides

For the King – the Cavaliers	For Parliament – the Roundheads
Lords	MPs
Landowners	Merchants
Anglicans	Puritans

Families split

Many families were split over which side to be on. Fathers fought sons, and brothers fought brothers.

Weapons

Most of the fighting in the Civil War was hand to hand. The main weapons were:

Muskets

Swords

Pikes

Cannon

Charles beaten

The Civil War lasted until 1646. Charles I lost the war. He gave himself up to the Scots. The Scots handed him over to Parliament.

Why did Parliament win the Civil War?

There were four reasons why Parliament won:

1 Parliament had better generals

The Royalists' best general was Prince Rupert. He was very brave and dashing. His cavalry charged the enemy at top speed. But he sometimes acted rashly and also lost control of his men.

Parliament's best general was Oliver Cromwell. He made few mistakes and his soldiers always carried out orders.

Cromwell

Prince Rupert

Question

List four reasons why Parliament won the Civil War.

The main battles of the English Civil War.

Royalists

Parliamentarians

Edgehill October 1642	Draw
Newbury September 1643	Draw
Marston Moor July 1644	Victory for Parliament and Scots
Naseby June 1645	Victory for Parliament
Preston August 1648	Parliament smashes Royalists and Scots

2 Other kings did not help Charles

Charles hoped kings from other countries would help him to fight Parliament. But no other king joined him.

In 1644 the Scots sent 20,000 men to fight on Parliament's side. The Scots helped Parliament to win the Battle of Marston Moor.

3 Parliament had the New Model Army

In 1644 Oliver Cromwell and Sir Thomas Fairfax formed the New Model Army to fight for Parliament. The soldiers in it were:

- well trained
- disciplined
- well paid
- well equipped
- well fed.

The Royalists laughed at it and called it the *New Noddle Army*!

But they were wrong to laugh. The New Model Army was very strong. It beat the King's army at Naseby in 1645.

4 Charles ran out of money

Charles lost a lot of men at Naseby.

He did not have enough money to raise another army.

Parliament was given money by rich merchants.

Parliament was also better at collecting taxes than the King.

A modern painting of a Royalist charge at the Battle of Edgehill in 1642.

Source A

Parliament talks to Charles

In 1646 Parliament started to talk to Charles about the way England would be run. Parliament did not want to kill Charles.

The army takes a hand

Now the war was over, Parliament told the army to go home. But the soldiers would not go because their wages had not been paid.

Instead the army took Charles prisoner. Now the army started to talk to Charles about peace.

Charles cannot be trusted

The army thought the talks were going well. Then Charles escaped to the Isle of Wight (a small island off the south coast of England). From there he made a deal with the Scots.

The Scots agreed to fight for Charles. The army was furious. Charles had shown that he could not be trusted.

The Battle of Preston, 1648

At this battle, the Scots were beaten by Cromwell's New Model Army.

The army said that Charles was a traitor and should die.

What about Parliament?

Some Members of Parliament thought Charles should live. The army went to the Houses of Parliament and threw out those who were on Charles' side.

The MPs who were left were called the **Rump**.

Charles put on trial

The Rump of MPs said Charles should be put on trial.

At the trial, Charles would not take his hat off because he did not want to show respect. He said that the court did not have the power to put the King on trial.

The court said Charles was a traitor and a murderer.

Source A

The hat worn by John Bradshaw, the chief judge at Charles' trial. It was strengthened inside by metal.

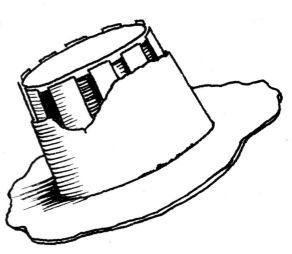

Source B

Over fifty judges signed Charles' death warrant. One of them was Oliver Cromwell. This is his signature.

Source C

The execution of Charles I in 1649.

Charles found guilty

Charles was found guilty by the court. John Bradshaw put on a red gown and told Charles that his head was to be chopped off.

Charles goes to his death

Charles was executed on 30 January 1649. It was very cold. He wore two shirts. He did not want the crowd to think he was shivering from fear.

Charles put his head on the block. His head was chopped off with one blow of the axe. People in the crowd were shocked by what they saw.

Questions

1 Read page 58. Write out these events in the order in which they happened:

- The Rump of MPs said Charles should be put on trial.
- Charles escaped from the army.
- Charles made a deal with the Scots.
- Charles was taken prisoner by the army.
- The army beat the Scots at the Battle of Preston.

2 Read **Charles put on trial**.

a What did the court say Charles had done?
b What did Charles say to the court?

3 Read **Charles found guilty**.

What did John Bradshaw do?

4 Look at Source A. Why do you think John Bradshaw's hat was strengthened with metal?

5 Read **Charles goes to his death**.

Why did Charles wear two shirts?

5.5 OLIVER CROMWELL: PROTECTOR OR DICTATOR?

England now a republic

England no longer had a king. It was now a **republic**. A republic is a country that does not have a king or queen.

Cromwell falls out with Parliament

Oliver Cromwell was now the most powerful person in the country. He was supported by the army.

Cromwell soon fell out with the Rump Parliament. In 1653 he went to the Houses of Parliament with some soldiers. All the Rump MPs were thrown out (see Sources A and B).

The Barebones Parliament

Cromwell and the army chose 140 new Members of Parliament. They were all Puritans.

They were called the **Barebones Parliament** after one of the MPs – Praise-God Barebones.

The MPs were not very good. They quarrelled with each other. Soon they said that they did not want to do the job any more.

Cromwell becomes Lord Protector

In 1653 the army made Cromwell the **Lord Protector** (ruler) of England.

Cromwell was not liked. He put up taxes.

Some people were worried that Cromwell and the army had too much power. Cromwell took action to stop these people grumbling.

Source A

Cromwell said this when he threw out the Rump MPs in 1653.

Go, I say. Let's have done with you. In the name of God, go!

Cromwell throws out the Rump MPs. Drawn by a Dutch artist.

Source B

The rule of the major-generals, 1655–1657

Cromwell put eleven army major-generals in charge. They were all strict Puritans. They stopped people enjoying themselves.

No theatres

No horse-racing

No festivities at Christmas

No bear-baiting

No drinking on Sundays

No swearing

The major-generals were very strict.

People hated the major-generals. Cromwell had to sack them in 1657.

Cromwell for king?

A lot of people thought England should have a king again. They asked Cromwell to be king, but he refused. He did not believe in kings. He had just fought a war to get rid of one!

Cromwell dies

Cromwell died in 1658. His son, Richard, became Lord Protector. He was so bad that he got the nickname 'Tumble-Down Dick'. Richard gave up after a year.

Source C

The Lord Protector
Ruled the people with Parliament and the Council.

The Council of State
Made up of civilian and army members. The Council helped the Lord Protector rule.

The people
Men who owned property worth more than £200 could vote.

£200

Women could not vote.

WHY CAN'T VOTE

How England was run when Cromwell was the Lord Protector.

Questions

1 Find Cromwell in Source B. What is he doing?

2 Read page 60. Copy these sentences. Fill in the gaps. Use the words in the box.

In _____ Cromwell became the _____ _____ of England.

The _____ ruled between 1655 and _____.

major-generals	Lord Protector
1657	1653

3 Read **The rule of the major-generals**.

Why were the major-generals hated?

The Civil War changed life in England. Many people said that the 'world had been turned upside down'.

The King had been executed and replaced by Cromwell, who was called the Lord Protector.

Ordinary people came up with ideas for running the country. They wrote leaflets and handed them out in the streets.

Who were these people and what ideas did they have?

Source A

The front cover of a leaflet called *The World Turned Upside Down*, printed in about 1647.

The Fifth Monarchists

This group believed that Jesus was about to come back to earth. He would then rule the earth as the 'fifth monarch'.

The Diggers

The Diggers were led by Gerrard Winstanley. They said everyone was equal. Everyone had an equal right to share and farm the land.

The Muggletonians

This group believed that God had given them the power to say who should go to Heaven and who should go to Hell. They were led by John Reeve and Ludowicke Muggleton.

The Levellers

The Levellers were led by John Lilburne. They wanted England to be run by Parliament, not a king. Most men would be able to vote for MPs, not just the rich. A lot of men in the army were Levellers.

The Quakers

The Quakers were started by George Fox in 1652. They believed that everyone was equal. They would not pay tithes (taxes) to the Church of England.

The Ranters

The Ranters believed they were God's chosen people. They said they could do nothing wrong.

Questions

Look at the drawings.

1 a Who was the leader of the Levellers?
b What did the Levellers want?

2 a Who was the leader of the Diggers?
b What did the Diggers say?

Who were the Levellers?

The Levellers were a group of soldiers in the New Model Army. This army was led by Cromwell. It fought on the side of Parliament in the Civil War.

The Levellers said Parliament should speak for everyone, not just the rich.

The Levellers fall out with Cromwell

The Levellers did not like Cromwell.

- They said he was only bothered about rich farmers.

- They were angry that the army's wages had not been paid.

- In 1649 some Levellers found out that Cromwell was sending them to fight in Ireland. They thought he was doing this to get them out of the way.

The march to Burford

The Levellers said that they would not let Cromwell treat them like this.

They mutinied and refused to go to Ireland.

They left the army and went on a march, picking up supporters on the way.

On 13 May 1649, they reached Burford in Oxfordshire.

Source A

This name was carved into the font in Burford church. Anthony Sedley was one of the Levellers trapped in the church by Cromwell.

Source B

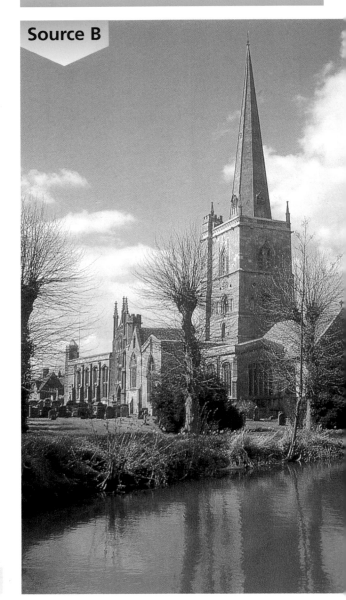

Burford church and churchyard.

Source C

From the Churchwardens' Account Book for Burford, 1649.

To Daniel Munke for cleaning the church when the Levellers were taken – 3s 6d [17.5p].

Cromwell attacks!

The Levellers set up camp for the night. But then they were attacked by a force led by Cromwell himself.

For three days, 340 Levellers were locked in Burford church. One of the Levellers carved his name on the font (see Source A).

The ringleaders executed

In the end, Cromwell had three of the ringleaders shot dead. The other Levellers were made to watch from the church roof.

Cromwell did not like the Levellers' ideas. By shooting the leaders, he was warning other people against following the Levellers.

Source D

From a leaflet written by the Levellers in 1649.

Cornet Den made an apology to Cromwell.

He said we were wrong and Cromwell was right.

Den howled and wept like a crocodile. He is a rogue and a villain.

The aims of the Levellers

The Levellers printed their aims in a leaflet in 1647.

- Parliament should meet every two years.

- Parliament should speak for everyone – not just the rich.

- All men should be allowed to vote (except servants and beggars).

- No more tithes (taxes) to the Church.

- People should be able to worship as they please.

Cornet Den

A fourth leader, called Cornet Den, should have been shot. But he begged Cromwell to forgive him.

Cromwell let him off.

The other Levellers were angry with Cornet Den. They said he was a rogue and a villain (see Source D).

Questions

1 Read page 64.

   a Who were the Levellers?
   b Why did the Levellers leave the army?

2 Read page 65. Why were the leaders shot?

Elizabeth's early life

Elizabeth Dysart was the daughter of William and Catherine Murray. Elizabeth was born in 1626.

The Murray family lived at Ham House in Surrey.

The Civil War

Charles I and William Murray were boyhood friends. Charles gave William a job in his government. William was on Charles' side in the Civil War.

William worked as a messenger for Charles. He carried letters to Charles' wife, who was living abroad. Charles made William the Count of Dysart as a reward.

After Charles I was executed in 1649, William fled to Holland.

Source A

Elizabeth Dysart as a young woman. She was known for her red hair.

Ham House. It was built in 1610 and is now owned by the National Trust.

Source B

Bishop Burnet said this about Elizabeth Dysart.

She was a clever woman, good at maths and history.

She was lively and chatty.

She was also friendly, but you would not want her for an enemy!

Friends with Cromwell

In 1648 Elizabeth married Sir Lionel Tollemache.

In the 1650s she became friendly with Oliver Cromwell, the Lord Protector of England. He visited Elizabeth's house. He liked her because she was witty and clever.

The Sealed Knot

Charles I's son, Charles Stuart, was living abroad in the 1650s. He wanted to return to England to be king. He had a lot of supporters in England.

The Sealed Knot was a secret society that smuggled letters to Charles. Elizabeth Dysart was in the Sealed Knot and carried its letters to Charles. It was dangerous work.

Source C

Elizabeth Dysart said this in 1658, when she heard that Cromwell had died.

All I can say is that I did know the 'old one'.

Source D

This was said of Elizabeth Dysart in 1677.

I went to see her at Ham House. She was very chatty. She was very beautiful when she was younger.

Was Elizabeth a double agent?

A double agent is someone who works for both sides at the same time. Some say Elizabeth was a double agent, working for both Cromwell and Charles Stuart.

Many historians say this is untrue:

1 Elizabeth and her family were strong supporters of the royal family. She probably would not have betrayed Charles Stuart.

2 Elizabeth's family was badly treated by Cromwell and Parliament in the Civil War. Parliament charged them heavy taxes and tried to take Ham House away from them.

Historians think Elizabeth made friends with Cromwell to cover up her membership of the Sealed Knot.

Charles II rewards Elizabeth

Charles Stuart returned to England in 1660. He became Charles II. He gave Elizabeth a pension of £800 as a reward for her help.

Questions

Read **Was Elizabeth a double agent?**

1 What is a double agent?

2 Do you think Elizabeth was a double agent? Give reasons for your answer.

5.9 FROM PROTECTOR TO THE ACT OF SETTLEMENT

England has a king again

Most people wanted to be ruled by a king again.

In 1660 Parliament asked Charles Stuart to come back to England as Charles II.

He arrived in England in May 1660. Crowds turned out to cheer him. They were pleased to have a king again.

It was called the **Restoration**.

A person who watched Charles II enter London wrote:

The roads were full of flowers. Bells were ringing.

There were trumpets and music.

There were so many people in the streets that it took seven hours to pass through the city.

Source A

Charles II, painted during his reign.

The merry monarch

Charles II was nicknamed 'The merry monarch'. This was because he liked having a good time.

He liked dancing, drinking wine and horse-racing. He was full of fun.

People were glad that the harsh rule of Cromwell was over.

Source B

Titus Oates in the pillory.

What was restored?

Charles II shows some mercy

Charles II did not want any more arguments. Most people who had fought against Charles I in the Civil War were pardoned.

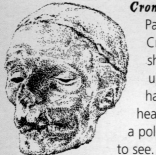

Cromwell's body

Parliament said that Cromwell's body should be dug up. The body was hanged. Then his head was stuck on a pole for everyone to see.

The Church of England

Parliament said the Church of England was once again the official religion. It was against the law to worship in other churches.

Laws against Catholics and Puritans

Parliament passed laws against Catholics and Puritans. They were not allowed to be Members of Parliament, councillors or teachers.

The Popish Plot, 1678

In 1678 Titus Oates told the government that Catholics were plotting to kill Charles II. He said they were going to make England Catholic again.

People panicked. Innocent Catholics were beaten up in the streets. Some Catholics were killed.

In the end, it was found that Oates had been lying. In 1685 he was sentenced to life imprisonment and to be flogged in public once a year. But he was let out of prison in 1689.

Source C

A description of Titus Oates being flogged in 1686.

Oates was flogged so hard that the crowd took pity on him.

They called out, 'Enough, enough! Be easy on him.'

Questions

1 Read **England has a king again**.

   a When did Charles II come back to England?

   b What was it like in London when Charles II arrived?

2 Read **The merry monarch**.

   Why was Charles II called 'the merry monarch'?

3 Read **What was restored?**

   What happened to Cromwell's body?

The death of Charles II

Charles II died in 1685. He was replaced by his brother, James II.

The Duke of Monmouth's rebellion, 1685

James II was a Catholic. He was hard working and a brave soldier. Many thought he would be a good king. Despite his religion, people thought he should be given a chance.

The Duke of Monmouth was the nephew of James II. Monmouth did not trust James II. Monmouth said he was the rightful king.

Monmouth led an army of rebels against James II. But they were not very well armed. They were badly beaten by James at the Battle of Sedgemoor in 1685.

Judge Jeffreys

The rebels were captured and put on trial. Judge Jeffreys was in charge. He was very hard on the rebels. Over 200 rebels were hanged and 800 sold to be slaves in the West Indies. The trials were called the **Bloody Assizes**.

James II makes himself unpopular

James II now allowed Catholics to join the army. This was against the law. James became unpopular. People began to think he was going to make England Catholic again.

James II's elder daughter, Mary, was due to become queen when he died.

People were glad about this because Mary was a Protestant. Her husband, William of Orange, was also a Protestant.

A baby boy arrives

Then, in 1688, James II's wife gave birth to a boy, James. This meant England would be ruled next by a Catholic king, not the Protestant Mary. Some people said the baby was smuggled into the queen's bedroom.

Source D

From a leaflet printed in London in 1679.

Catholic soldiers will attack your wives and daughters. They will hit your children's heads against walls and bash their brains out.

Catholics will steal from your houses and cut your throats.

This is what happened when England was ruled by Catholics before.

Source E

Sir Robert Walpole speaking to the Cabinet.

The Glorious Revolution, 1688

Parliament did not want England to have another Catholic ruler. So it asked William of Orange and Mary to rule England.

William arrived in England from Holland with a big army. He marched to London. James II fled to France.

Parliament had chosen the new king and queen. Historians often refer to this as the **Glorious Revolution**.

New laws

William and Mary were now the Protestant King and Queen. They agreed to new laws.

The new laws meant that Parliament would now have more say in running the country. The power of the King was cut down.

The new laws that cut down the King's power.

No taxation without Parliament's consent

No army in peace time

Freedom of speech for MPs

No Catholic monarch

Parliament to meet at least every 3 years

Queen Anne and George I

Mary died in 1694 and William died in 1702. Queen Anne became the next ruler. She died in 1714 without any children.

James I's great grandson took over. He was George I and he came from Hanover in Germany.

Robert Walpole

Robert Walpole became the first Prime Minister. He led a group of other ministers called the **Cabinet**. The Prime Minister talked to the King about running the country.

Questions

1 Read **New laws**.

   Who had more power after 1688: the King or Parliament?

2 Read **Robert Walpole**.

   Who was Robert Walpole?

The Pale

In 1500 most of Ireland was run by Irish princes.

The Irish people had their own language (**Gaelic**) and their own laws. They were Catholics.

The English ruled some land around Dublin. This land was called the Pale.

Henry VIII (1509–1547) and Ireland

Henry VIII said he was the King of Ireland.

During his reign, England broke away from the Catholic Church.

England became a Protestant country.

Henry VIII wanted Ireland to become Protestant. But the Irish wanted to stay Catholics. They rebelled against Henry.

Elizabeth I (1558–1603) and Ireland

Elizabeth I took land away from the Irish rebels.

She gave their land to Protestant **settlers** from England who went to live in Ireland.

This was called **plantation**. The Irish were very angry about it.

The Irish rebel again

In 1595 the Irish raised an army to fight the English.

Elizabeth I was furious. She sent an army to Ireland.

The fighting was fierce, but the English won.

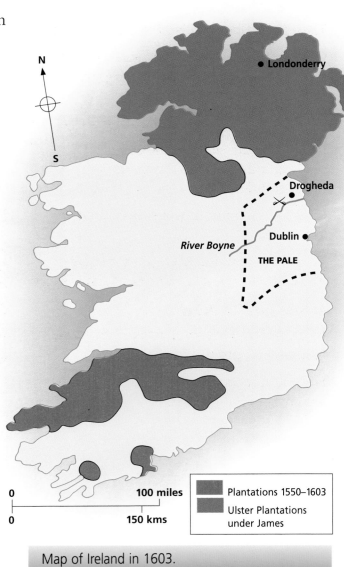

N
S

Londonderry

Drogheda

River Boyne

Dublin

THE PALE

| 0 | | 100 miles |
| 0 | | 150 kms |

Plantations 1550–1603
Ulster Plantations under James

Map of Ireland in 1603.

James I (1603–1625) and Ireland

James I did not trust the Irish. He thought they might cause trouble for England.

In 1607 James I sent more Protestant settlers to **Ulster**, the northern part of Ireland.

This was called the **Ulster Plantation**. They took the best farming land away from the Irish.

Cromwell and Drogheda, 1649

In 1641 Irish Catholics rebelled against the English.

They killed thousands of Protestant settlers.

Oliver Cromwell was a Puritan. He did not like Catholics. He wanted to stop the Irish Catholics rebelling.

He went to Ireland with a strong army.

In 1649 he lay siege to the town of Drogheda. But the town would not surrender.

Cromwell's cannon broke through the town walls.

Then his men murdered 3,000 people inside the town. It was a terrible **massacre**.

More land taken

In the 1650s, Cromwell took even more land away from the Irish Catholics.

He sent hundreds of Irish rebels to work as slaves in the West Indies.

Source A

Cromwell said this about the massacre at Drogheda.

Killing lots of Irish people in Drogheda was God's wish. It will stop any more bloodshed in the future.

Source B

This picture of Irish Catholics killing Protestants was drawn in 1841. It made things look worse than they really were.

James II goes to France

In 1688 the Catholic James II fled to France. He was replaced by the Protestant William III and his wife Mary.

James II goes to Ireland

From France, James II went to Ireland. There he helped the Irish Catholics.

He took land from the Protestant settlers and gave it back to the Irish Catholics.

The siege of Londonderry, 1689

Londonderry was a Protestant city. James II raised an army and tried to capture the city.

But the people of Londonderry closed the gates and would not let James in.

James lay siege to the city for sixteen weeks. His army camped outside the city and would not let any food in. He wanted to starve the people into surrender.

William III sends food to Londonderry

William III did not want James to control Ireland. So he sent warships full of food to Londonderry. Source D tells what happened.

Source C

This painting is on a wall in Londonderry. It was done by a Protestant in the 1980s. William III is shown winning the Battle of the Boyne in 1690.

Source D

The siege of Londonderry, by a person who was inside the city.

James II arrived outside the city on 12 April 1689. We would not surrender to him. His army camped outside the city walls.

During May and June, James attacked the city. One night bombs were put under the walls. Seven people were blown to pieces.

We were short of food. People started to eat horses and dogs. They also drank horses' blood because there was so little water.

Thousands of people starved to death.

In the end we were saved by William III, who sent some warships with food.

The Battle of the Boyne, 1690.

The Battle of the Boyne, 1690

William III was frightened that James II was taking control of Ireland. In 1690 William went to Ireland with an army.

On 1 July 1690, William and James fought a battle at the river Boyne. The fighting went on all day. William won the battle.

James fled from Ireland and went back to France for safety.

After the battle

The English stopped the Catholics from voting or having jobs in the government. Ireland was under the control of English Protestants. It was a conquered land.

Londonderry

William III defeated James II 1690

IRELAND

Battle of the Boyne

Dublin

James II landed here 1689

Limerick

Questions

1 Read page 72.

Copy these sentences. Fill in the gaps, using the words in the box.

Ireland was a ____ country. England was a ____ country. ____ wanted to make Ireland a Protestant country.

____ took land from the Irish and gave it to the English. This was called ____.

plantation	Catholic
Henry VIII	Elizabeth I
Protestant	

2 Read page 75.

What happened at the Battle of the Boyne?

6.2 SCOTLAND AND ENGLAND: A UNION OF KINGDOMS?

Scotland – a separate country

Before 1603 England and Scotland were separate countries. They often fought wars against each other.

Highlanders and Lowlanders

There were two main groups in Scotland:

1 The Highlanders

They lived in northern Scotland and were mostly Catholic. They were divided into big families called **clans**.

2 The Lowlanders

They lived in the south of Scotland. They were mostly Protestant.

James VI and James I

In 1603 King James VI of Scotland became King James I of England. The two countries now shared the same king.

But Scotland still had its own Parliament, law courts and Church.

Cromwell and Scotland

Charles I was executed in 1649. The Scots wanted his son to become Charles II. They gave him an army to fight Cromwell.

In 1651 Charles and the Scots were beaten by Cromwell in the Battle of Worcester. Charles fled to Europe.

Then Cromwell sent an army to Scotland. He closed down the Scottish Parliament and Church. Scotland was now being ruled by the English.

William III and Scotland

In 1688 the Catholic James II was forced to run away to France.

The new king was a Protestant, William III.

The Highlanders hated him. William made the Highlanders sign an oath of loyalty to him. Trouble followed!

The Massacre of Glencoe 1692

The MacDonalds, one of the Highland clans, were six days late in signing the oath of loyalty. That gave William an excuse to punish the Highlanders for being on the side of James II.

In 1692 William sent soldiers to Glencoe, where the MacDonalds lived. The soldiers were friendly for two weeks.

Then one night the soldiers attacked the MacDonalds. The chief and thirty-seven of his clan were murdered. Others ran away across the mountains and died from the cold.

It was an act of terrible cruelty. The Highlanders now hated the English more than ever.

Why did Scotland join with England?

England was much richer than Scotland.

If Scotland joined with England, it could trade with England's **colonies**. This would make the Scots richer.

The Act of Union, 1707

In 1707 Scotland and England joined together. They were now called the **United Kingdom**.

Scotland gave up its own Parliament. Instead it sent forty-five MPs to the British Parliament in London.

It was the Lowland Scots who agreed the Act of Union with England.

The Highlanders did not want to join with England.

Trouble was brewing once again.

The Jacobites

The Highlanders wanted James Edward Stuart as their king. He was the son of James II and a Catholic.

Supporters of James were called **Jacobites** (*Jacobus* is Latin for James).

In 1714 Queen Anne died. The Jacobites thought that James Edward Stuart would be made king.

Instead the throne went to George I of Hanover. The Jacobites were furious.

Questions

1 What were the two main groups of people in Scotland?

2 Read **Why did Scotland join with England?**

Write down a reason why Scotland joined with England.

3 When was the Act of Union?

The Act of Union, 1707

The Scots agreed that:

- there would be one Parliament for the new United Kingdom. It would be held in London.

The English agreed that:

- the Scots could keep their own Church and law courts.

The Jacobites rebel, 1715

The Jacobites raised an army to put James Edward Stuart on the throne. But they were not very well organised.

The Jacobites were easily beaten in a battle near Stirling. They went back to the mountains. The rebellion was over.

The Jacobites rebel again, 1745

In 1745 James Edward Stuart's son, Charles, landed in Scotland. He was nicknamed 'Bonnie Prince Charlie'.

He said his father was the rightful king. Many Highlanders joined his army.

Bonnie Prince Charlie marches into England

Bonnie Prince Charlie marched into England with an army of 5,000 men. He wanted the English Catholics to join up with him. But very few did.

Bonnie Prince Charlie reached Derby and then turned back to Scotland.

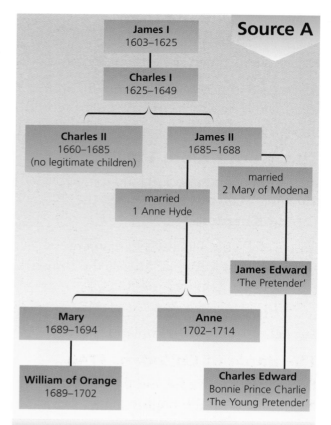

The family tree of the Stuarts. The dates given are the dates they reigned.

Bonnie Prince Charlie. He died a drunkard in 1788.

Retreat

Advance of Bonnie Prince Charlie

The Battle of Culloden, painted in 1746. The artist was paid by the Duke of Cumberland.

The Battle of Culloden, 1746

Bonnie Prince Charlie and the Jacobites were chased by the English army.

The English were led by the Duke of Cumberland. He caught up with the Jacobites at Culloden in the north of Scotland. The Jacobites were tired, cold and hungry.

There was a bloody battle. The Jacobites were massacred. As the Jacobites ran from the battlefield, Cumberland's men hacked them to death. The Scots nicknamed Cumberland 'The Butcher' because he was so cruel.

Bonnie Prince Charlie escaped to France.

What happened to the Highlanders?

The English sent soldiers to the Highlands so there would not be another rebellion. A lot of Highlanders were driven from their homes. Some went to America.

Scotland gets richer

By 1800 Scotland had grown richer.

Cotton factories were set up in the Lowlands.

Glasgow became a busy port.

Questions

1 Read **The Jacobites** on page 77.

   Who were the Jacobites?

2 Read page 78.

   a In which two years did the Jacobites rebel?
   b Who led the second rebellion?

3 Read **The Battle of Culloden, 1746**.

   What happened in the battle?

Witches

During the 1500s and 1600s, people were very superstitious. They did not know much about science. If something went wrong, people said it was the work of the Devil. People believed that the Devil's work was carried out by **witches**.

What was a witch?

People (usually women) were thought to be witches if they:

- were quite old
- had marks on their bodies
- kept a cat
- lived alone and did not mix
- were poor.

People said that witches got their powers from evil spirits and the Devil.

What were witches supposed to do?

People believed that witches could:

- turn a cow's milk sour
- make horses go lame
- cause storms and make ships sink
- turn children blind.

Doing things like this was called **witchcraft**.

Hunt the witch!

In 1563 Parliament said that witchcraft was against the law. Anyone found guilty of being a witch would be hanged.

Some people became 'official' witch-hunters. The most famous was Matthew Hopkins. He called himself the 'Witch-finder General'. If a woman was thought to be a witch, she was tied up and thrown into a pond. If she floated, she was guilty; if she sank, she was innocent.

Witch hunting ended in the 1750s. By then people did not believe in witches as much.

Source A

Witches standing inside a magic circle. They are sweari[ng] loyalty to the Devil.

Source B

This vicar did not want Matthew Hopkins in his village.

Every old woman with wrinkles, a hairy lip, a squinting eye and a squeaky voice will be called a witch by him.

Did you know?

Many thought Anne Boleyn, Henry VIII's second wife, was a witch. This was because she had three nipples and an extra finger.

The story of old Mother Osborne

In 1751, Ruth Osborne was accused of being a witch.

Source C

A report in a magazine, April 1751.

At Tring in Hertfordshire, an innkeeper said that Ruth Osborne was a witch.

A mob got hold of Ruth Osborne. She was:

- **stripped naked and her thumbs were tied to her toes**

- **dragged two miles to a muddy stream**

- **ducked in the stream**

- **called names.**

Ruth Osborne choked with mud and died.

Source D

From a letter to the same magazine, June 1751.

Some time ago an old woman called Osborne begged a farmer for some milk.

The farmer said he did not have any milk to give her.

The old woman was angry. She told him the Devil would have his cows.

Afterwards some of his cows became ill. Some stupid people then said Osborne was a witch.

Thomas Colley was arrested for the murder of Ruth Osborne. He was found guilty and hanged in chains.

The ducking of Ruth Osborne.

Source F

This is what Thomas Colley said before he was hanged.

I murdered Ruth Osborne because I was drunk. I do not believe that there is such a thing as a witch.

Questions

1 Read **Witches**.

   Why did people in the 1500s and 1600s believe in witches?

2 Read **What were witches supposed to do?**

   Make a list of things people thought witches could do.

3 Read Source C.

   What happened to Ruth Osborne?

4 Read Source D and Source F.

   Was Ruth really a witch? Explain your answer.

The plague strikes, 1665

The year 1665 was terrible. The plague struck England. It was a horrible illness (see the box below). Over 110,000 people died in London alone.

What people thought caused the plague

People had different ideas about what caused the plague. They said it was caused by:

- dry, warm weather
- poisonous gases
- too many dogs
- God's anger.

Some people even thought that the plague was spread by Jews and Catholics.

The microscope had not been invented in 1665. People did not know that disease was caused by germs in the air.

Prevention and treatment

As people did not know what caused the plague, they had little idea of how to stop it spreading.

They also had few ideas about how to prevent or treat it. Some of their ideas are shown on page 83.

What was 'the plague'?

The main type of plague was called the **bubonic plague**.

The plague was sometimes called the Black Death.

The plague was caused by germs.

These germs were spread by fleas that lived on rats.

The germs were passed on to people if they were bitten by the fleas.

What was it like to have the plague?

Large lumps (called **buboes**) grew under the armpit and in the groin.

These lumps were the size of a chicken's egg.

The lumps were very painful. They turned black and were full of poison.

Then people got a pink rash.

After that, people got a high temperature and a fever.

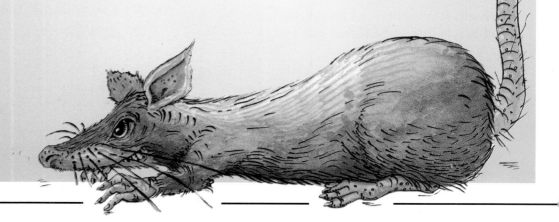

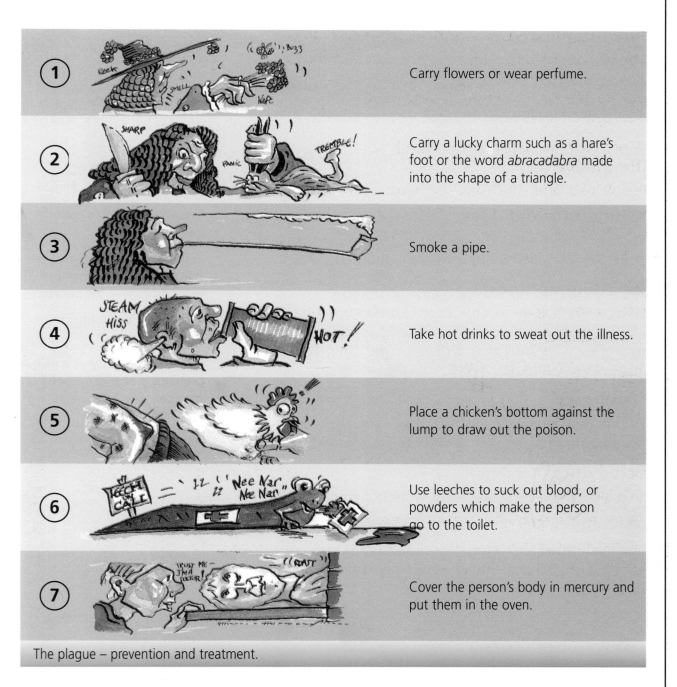

①	Carry flowers or wear perfume.
②	Carry a lucky charm such as a hare's foot or the word *abracadabra* made into the shape of a triangle.
③	Smoke a pipe.
④	Take hot drinks to sweat out the illness.
⑤	Place a chicken's bottom against the lump to draw out the poison.
⑥	Use leeches to suck out blood, or powders which make the person go to the toilet.
⑦	Cover the person's body in mercury and put them in the oven.

The plague – prevention and treatment.

Questions

1 Read **What people thought caused the plague**.

   a What did people think caused the plague?
   b Why didn't they know the real cause?

2 Look at the box on page 82. What was it like to have the plague?

3 Look at the chart above. Do you think any of these ways of stopping the plague helped?

What happened in London in 1665?

The plague arrived in London in the spring of 1665.

When the summer came, the number of deaths shot up.

People lived in dirty, crowded houses. The warm weather helped the germs to spread.

Rich people moved out of London into the countryside.

Charles II moved away to Oxford.

Killing cats and dogs

Many people thought the plague was spread by cats and dogs. So they killed thousands of them.

Boarding up houses

Houses that had the plague were boarded up. A red cross was painted on the door to warn people. The words *Lord, have mercy upon us* were written on the door. The families inside were left to die.

Watchmen

Two **watchmen** kept watch on the houses that were boarded up to make sure none of the family left.

Bring out your dead!

So many people died that there were not enough coffins.

At night, men took carts around the streets of London.

The men called out 'Bring out your dead!' Bodies were put on to these carts and taken to be buried in big pits.

The pits were quickly filled in.

Source A

Samuel Pepys lived in London during the plague. He kept a diary of what happened. He wrote this in September 1665.

In one week, over 6,000 people died from the plague.

There is no one to be seen on the streets.

I cannot get any food that is safe to eat. My butcher and baker both have the plague.

No one will buy a wig at the moment.

People are scared that it has been made from the hair of someone who has died of the plague.

Questions

Read Source A.

1 Write down two things which show that people were scared of the plague.
2 Would you trust what Samuel Pepys says? Explain your answer.

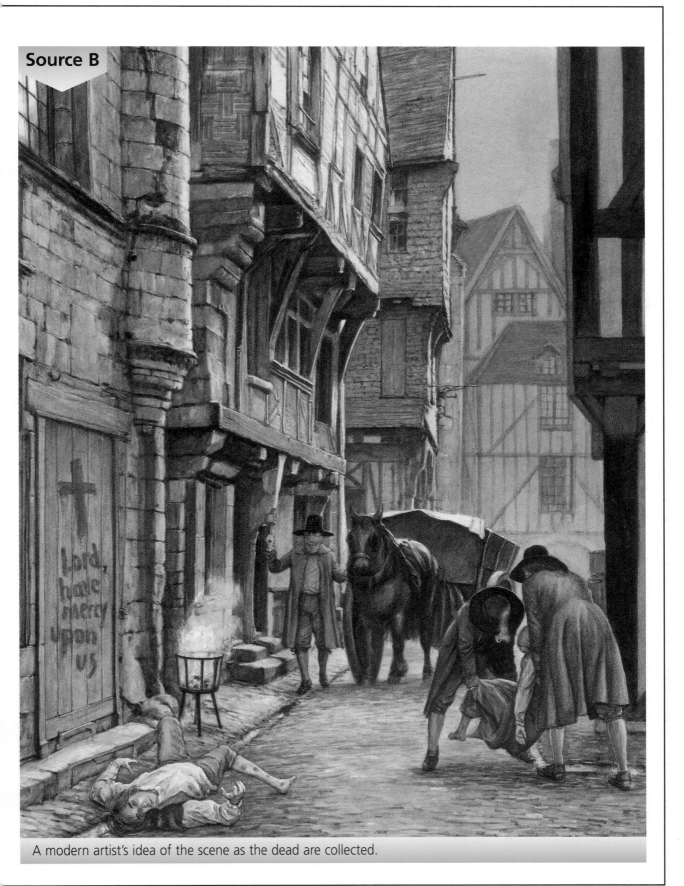

A modern artist's idea of the scene as the dead are collected.

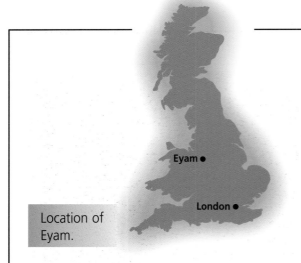

Location of Eyam.

Other places

There were outbreaks of the plague all over England. Ports such as Southampton and Newcastle were badly hit.

Eyam – 'The Plague Village'
George Vicars

Eyam is a small village in Derbyshire. One day in 1665, a parcel of cloth from London was delivered to George Vicars, the local tailor. Within two days, George fell ill and before long he was dead. He had caught the dreaded plague.

William Mompesson

William Mompesson was the Vicar of Eyam. He said no one should leave the village. If people left, they would spread the plague to other places.

The local people stayed in Eyam. Food was left outside the village for collection. Soon people began to die.

People were scared to go to church, in case they caught the plague from someone else. So William held his services in the open air.

Many deaths

The plague killed 267 of the 350 people who lived in Eyam. One of the last to die was Catherine Mompesson, the vicar's wife.

The villagers, though, had been very brave. They stayed in Eyam, even though they knew they would probably get the plague.

By staying in Eyam, they had not spread the plague to other villages.

The end of the plague

When the cold winter weather came, fewer people died of the plague. The plague was finally ended by the Great Fire of London in 1666. The fire killed the rats, fleas and germs that had brought the plague.

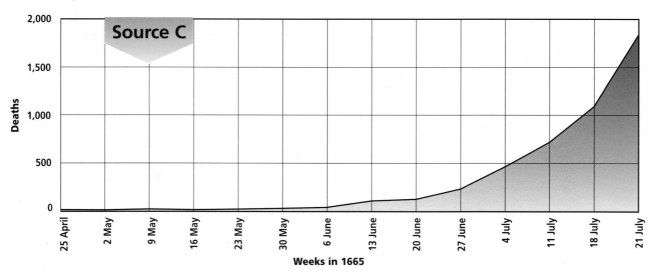

Source C

SAMUEL PEPYS

Samuel Pepys worked for the navy.

Pepys kept a diary. His diary tells us a lot about life in the 1660s.

He tell us about:

- the return of Charles II in 1660
- the plague in 1665
- the Great Fire of London in 1666.

Without Pepys' diary we would not know as much as we do about the 1660s.

Pepys died in 1703.

Source D

Daniel Defoe writing about the plague in 1722.

People would climb out of windows in front of the watchmen.

About twenty watchmen were shot trying to stop people escaping from houses that had been shut [boarded] up.

Deaths in London from April to July 1665.

Questions

1 Read **George Vicars**.

  a Where is Eyam?
  b What happened to George Vicars?

2 Read **William Mompesson**.

  a Who was William?
  b What did he say to the villagers?
  c How did the villagers get their food?

3 Read **Many deaths**.

  a How many people died in Eyam?
  b What was so brave about what they did?

Source A

The Great Fire of London. The artist saw the fire happen.

Source B

From Samuel Pepys' diary. He lived in London at the time of the fire.

I saw the fire raging.

No one could put it out.

Churches and houses were all on fire.

The flames made an awful noise.

I saw a cat with all the hair burned off its body. But it was still alive!

Fire!

On 2 September 1666, a fire started in a bakery in Pudding Lane, London. It was only a small fire to begin with.

The fire spreads

A strong wind was blowing. The fire suddenly took hold and spread quickly.

The houses were made of wood, so they burned down easily.

There was not much people could do.

The end of the fire

The Great Fire of London lasted for three days. It did a lot of damage. The fire burned down:

- 89 churches
- 13,200 houses
- 400 streets.

Who started the fire?

People thought the fire had been started on purpose.
They were sure a foreigner or a Catholic had started it.

Source C

From Samuel Pepys' diary.

Some people are saying that Catholics started the fire on purpose.
They say Catholics boasted that the hot, dry weather was just right
for starting a fire.

Source D

Written by a modern historian.

In October 1666, Robert Hubert was executed for starting the
fire. Hubert was born in France. He was thought to be a Catholic.
He admitted starting the fire, but later said he was lying. Hubert
arrived in England two days after the fire started. So he could
not have started it!

This column is called the Monument. It was built in 1669 near
to the spot where the fire started. At the bottom it says that
Catholics started the fire.

The Monument was built by Sir Christopher Wren. He also
rebuilt a lot of other buildings, including St Paul's Cathedral.

Source F

A modern historian explains
why the fire was so bad.

The wind was strong.
The water pump near
London Bridge was broken.

The weather had been
very dry. The wells had
no water in them.

Questions

1 Read **Fire!**

   Where did the fire start?

2 Read **The fire spreads** and **The end of the fire**.

   a How much damage did the fire do?
   b Why did the fire do so much damage?

3 Read Source D.

   Why could Robert Hubert **not** have started the fire?

Colonies

Between 1603 and 1750, Britain captured lots of different bits of land across the world. These pieces of land were called **colonies**. All the colonies together made up the **British Empire**.

Trading companies

Trading companies were made up of merchants. Most colonies were started by these trading companies.

The merchants wanted to build up trade and make money.

- From North America they brought furs.
- From the East Indies they brought spices, tea and dyes.
- From the West Indies they brought cotton, tobacco, rum and sugar.

The merchants made money by selling these goods in Britain.

British factories made money by selling cloth, pans, guns and nails to the colonies.

London, Glasgow, Liverpool and Bristol became very busy ports.

Settlers

Many British people went to settle (live) in the new colonies.

Why people went to the colonies

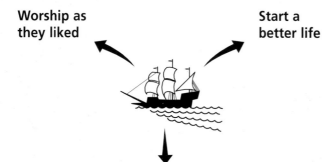

Worship as they liked

Start a better life

Plenty of land to farm

Some colonies gained by Britain, 1655–1713

- Jamaica
- Gibraltar
- Newfoundland
- Nova Scotia
- Hudson's Bay

Source A

A settler tells what America was like in 1620.

The land was empty. There were many wild animals. It was very dangerous.

Source B

Bristol in 1720. The slave trade made Bristol a rich port.

Source C

A cargo ship being built in the East India Company's dockyard on the River Thames.

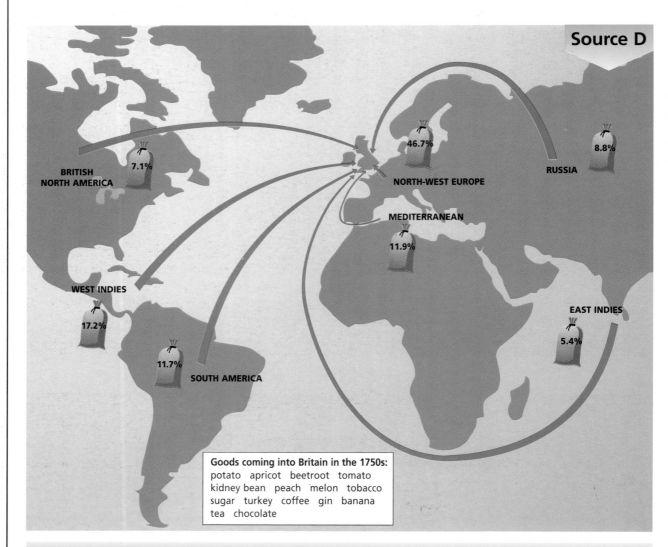

BRITISH
NORTH AMERICA
7.1%

WEST INDIES
17.2%

SOUTH AMERICA
11.7%

NORTH-WEST EUROPE
46.7%

RUSSIA
8.8%

MEDITERRANEAN
11.9%

EAST INDIES
5.4%

Goods coming into Britain in the 1750s:
potato apricot beetroot tomato
kidney bean peach melon tobacco
sugar turkey coffee gin banana
tea chocolate

In the 1750s, lots of goods were being brought to Britain from all over the world. The percentages show the amount of goods coming from each country.

The slave trade

Some merchants made lots of money out of the cruel slave trade.

How the slave trade worked

1 Ships full of pots, pans and guns sailed to Africa. These goods were traded for black slaves.

2 Then the ships sailed to the West Indies. There, the slaves were traded for rum, sugar, tobacco and cotton. The slaves were made to work in the fields.

Their lives were hard and they often had cruel masters.

3 The ships sailed back to Britain. The rum, sugar, tobacco and cotton was sold.

Sugar fetched very good prices. It was used to sweeten tea, coffee, cakes and puddings.

The slave traders made huge amounts of money. They built themselves big houses to live in.

A coffee house in London in the 1700s. Merchants and businessmen met here to drink coffee and set up business deals. They also chatted about the news of the day. There were about 600 coffee houses in London.

Source F

An advert in a London newspaper, 1728.

For sale: A black boy, aged eleven. Apply at the Virginia Coffee House in London.

Source G

Written by Daniel Defoe in the 1720s.

Merchants in Bristol trade with places all over the world.

Questions

1 Read **Colonies** on page 90 then write out these sentences, filling in the gaps.

Between _____ and _____ Britain captured bits of land across the world. These pieces of land were called _____.

2 Look at the box on page 90. List three of Britain's colonies.

3 Read **Trading companies** on page 90.

a What goods did Britain get from:
- North America   • the East Indies
- the West Indies?

b Find these places on the map on page 92.

4 Read page 92.

Which trade earned lots of money for British merchants?

5 Look at Source E. What can we learn from this source about life in the 1700s?

Source A

The coronation of King Charles II in 1660.

Who was Daniel Defoe?

There were many parts to Daniel Defoe. He was:

- a reporter
- a spy
- a merchant
- a story-teller.

Daniel's childhood

Daniel was born in London in 1660 – the same year that Charles II was made king (see Source A). Daniel's father was a candle merchant called James Foe. He wanted Daniel to be a vicar. But Daniel had other ideas!

Merchant and factory owner

Daniel became a stocking merchant. He travelled all over Europe, but he lost a lot of money. He started up a brick factory. This, too, lost money.

Daniel changes his name

In 1695 Daniel got a job with the government. He changed his surname from Foe to Defoe. Perhaps he thought it was more posh!

Daniel gets into trouble

Daniel now did something very silly.

He started to write leaflets that poked fun at the Church of England. He also wrote bad things about the government.

Daniel was sent to prison for this.

When Daniel came out of prison, he started working as a **spy** for the government.

Source B

A
TOUR
Thro' the whole ISLAND of
GREAT BRITAIN,
Divided into
Circuits or Journies.
GIVING

A Particular and Diverting Account of Whatever is Curious and worth Observation, Viz.

I. A Description of the Principal Cities and Towns, their Situation, Magnitude, Government, and Commerce.
II. The Customs, Manners, Speech, as also the Exercises, Diversions, and Employment of the People.
III. The Produce and Improvement of the Lands, the Trade, and Manufactures.
IV. The Sea Ports and Fortifications, the Course of Rivers, and the Inland Navigation.
V. The Publick Edifices, Seats, and Palaces of the Nobility and Gentry.

With Useful Observations upon the Whole.

Particularly fitted for the Reading of such as desire to Travel over the ISLAND.

By a GENTLEMAN.

LONDON:
Printed, and Sold by G. Strahan, in Cornhill.
W. Mears, at the Lamb without Temple-Bar.
R. Francklin, under Tom's Coffee-house, Covent-Garden.
S. Chapman, at the Angel in Pall-Mall.
R. Stagg, in Westminster-Hall, and
J. Graves, in St. James's-Street. MDCCXXIV.

The title page of one of Defoe's books, written in the 1720s.

Daniel the story-teller

In 1704 Daniel started writing story books. His most famous book was about a ship-wrecked sailor called *Robinson Crusoe*.

He also wrote the story of *Moll Flanders*.

Daniel writes about the plague of 1665

In 1722 Daniel wrote a book about the plague of 1665.

Daniel was only five at the time of the plague, so he would not have remembered much about it.

He wrote his book from stories that his uncle had told him.

Daniel writes about Britain

In 1724 Daniel wrote a book called *A Tour Through the Whole Island of Great Britain* (see Source B).

He said he went all around Britain and wrote down what he saw.

But Daniel did not go to all the places that are in the book.

He used information from other people and some that he made up!

Daniel Defoe died in 1731.

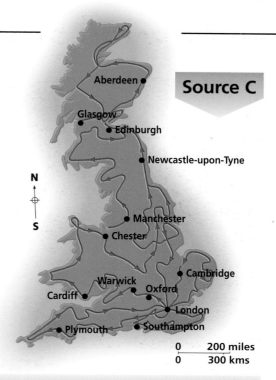

Source C

Some of the places in Britain that Defoe said he had been to on his 'Tour'.

Source D

What Defoe wrote about Warwick.

The church, town hall and gaol are all new buildings. They are the finest of any town in England.

The George Inn on the corner of the High Street looks like a palace.

There are four horse markets here each year.

Questions

1 Look at Source A. What happened in the same year that Daniel was born?

2 Read **Who was Daniel Defoe?**

   List four things that Daniel did in his life.

3 Read **Daniel the story-teller**.

   Name two famous stories written by Daniel.

4 Read **Daniel writes about Britain**.

   Do you believe what Daniel says Britain was like in 1724? Explain your answer.

INDEX